# Gerald Sambrooke-Sturgess

# The Rules in Action

SAIL Books
Boston

Copyright © G. Sambrooke-Sturgess 1982
First published in the United States by

SAIL Books
34 Commercial Wharf
Boston, MA 02110

ISBN 0-914814-39-7

SAIL Books are published by Sail Publications, Inc.

LIBRARY OF CONGRESS CATALOGING IN
PUBLICATION DATA

Sambrooke-Sturgess, Gerald.
    The rules in action.

    Includes index.
    1. Yacht racing—Rules—Addresses, essays, lectures.
I. Title.
GV826.7.S25   1982   797.1ʹ4      82-10814
ISBN 0-914814-39-7

# Contents

# Preface

I have been persuaded to write this book by the number of readers of *Yachts and Yachting* who have suggested that my articles be reproduced in more permanent form, an idea that the Editor, Peter Cook, supported. I have often been encouraged to learn from readers that many of them have cut out and filed these pieces, together with the earlier ones which appeared in *Yachting World* up to 1979. It should be understood that this is not a comprehensive exposition of the yacht racing rules, but a collection of pieces on subjects that have arisen in appeals and questions to the Racing Rules Committee of the Royal Yachting Association, in letters from readers, and in talks with fellow yachtsmen over the years.

I must thank the Council of the RYA, and the Executive Committees of the International Yacht Racing Union and the United States Yacht Racing Union for kindly allowing me to quote their case law, in my attempt to help readers to a better understanding of the spirit and letter of the rules. I am greatly indebted to Peter Cook for his interest in and generous support of this project, particularly in supplying tear sheets and art work for the various pieces.

G S-S

# 1 Simple Really

At first glance the racing rules of the International Yacht Racing Union (IYRU) appear complex. They include 2 definitions, 78 rules and 10 appendices. In addition the national authority of each country adds a number of its own prescriptions, and in the UK this is the Royal Yachting Association (RYA), which publishes the complete rules and prescriptions together in its booklet YR1/81.

The newcomer to the sport may therefore quite understandably feel daunted at apparently having to master so much detail but, although he would obviously be well advised to understand all the rules, in fact, to compete in a race he need not do so at the outset.

The rules are arranged in the chronological order in which they become effective and are grouped in six parts:

I—**Definitions**, which enable the rules to be written much more concisely.

II—**Management of Races**, which tell the race committee and the competitors how races must be run.

III—**General Requirements**, which explain the obligations of the owner of a yacht or dinghy (the rules do not differentiate) who seeks to qualify her to enter a race.

IV—**Right-of-Way Rules**, which govern the manoeuvres of yachts while racing, and state which yacht must keep clear of another.

V—**Other Sailing Rules**, which set out the obligations of helmsmen and crews in handling their yachts.

VI—**Protests, Penalties and Appeals**, which detail the procedures to be followed when protesting, hearing and deciding protests, and lodging appeals.

Hence, in order to compete in a race, it is really only essential to grasp and to apply the broad principles of the basic right-of-way rules in Part IV. If the novice does this, he can expect to keep out of trouble himself and to avoid interfering illegally with his fellow competitors, to the great relief of all concerned.

What, then, are these basic principles?

The rules are designed to fulfil three requirements. First, to enable yachts to manoeuvre at close quarters, i.e. to avoid collision. In theory, *there should never be a collision under the right-of-way rules*. In practice, however, when a yacht that should have kept clear fails to do so, the right-of-way yacht is not prohibited from just touching the offender to stress the fact that the give-way yacht did not keep clear. Secondly, to ensure that yachts compete equitably against each other. Thirdly, to be educational, for it is important to appreciate that the rules apply to all types and sizes of boats, sailing offshore, inshore and on inland waters, in all kinds of wind, weather and tide.

It follows that in normal conditions when two boats touch while racing, one of them must have infringed a right-of-way rule and should be penalised unless, after hearing a protest, the race committee finds that the contact was minor and in the circumstances unavoidable; this is not a matter for the two helmsmen to decide themselves.

Some sailors quite wrongly believe that it is unsporting to protest. Because it is impracticable for a race committee to police the whole racing area for possible rule infringements, the competitors themselves are required to ensure a strict observance of the rules by protesting against any yacht that infringes them. A competitor who infringes a rule and is not penalised will obtain points and a place in that race to which he is not entitled, which is unfair on other helmsmen who have carefully observed the rules. Enjoyment of racing depends on the attitude of the competitors towards strict rule observance, and certain classes are notorious for their flagrant disregard of the rules.

The first rule of the book, the Fundamental Fair Sailing rule, makes it clear that a yacht shall compete in a race only by fair sailing, superior speed and skill. In other words, trying to win a race by knowingly infringing a rule is cheating, and this is quite foreign to the whole concept of the sport. Consequently, when a yacht knowingly infringes a rule, she should immediately either retire or, if an alternative penalty applies, exonerate herself. If she does neither and persists in racing, the other yachts should protest against her, but nevertheless they must continue to accord her such rights as she may have under the rules of Part IV.

Again, from a safety point of view, a yacht should hail another yacht when making an unforeseen alteration of course and when claiming an overlap at a mark or obstruction.

In the interests of both safety and equity, a right-of-way yacht is prohibited from altering course in such a manner as to prevent the give-way yacht from keeping clear, or so as to obstruct her while she is keeping clear, except in three special situations which are specified in rule 35 (Limitations on Altering Course). It should not be difficult to understand and apply these principles, as they are based on common sense and fair play.

Turning now specifically to the rules governing the right of way between two approaching yachts, they are framed to cover the four basic positional relationships that can exist between them.

(i) On opposite tacks – port-tack yacht keeps clear.

(ii) On same tack – windward yacht keeps clear.

(iii) One or both yachts are changing tacks, either by tacking or gybing – the yacht which is changing tacks keeps clear, unless both do so simultaneously, when the one on the other's port side keeps clear.

(iv) One yacht is anchored, aground or capsized – the yacht under way keeps clear.

These right-of-way rules are subject to modifications of three kinds:

(a) There are some exceptions to the basic rules.

(b) There are some limitations on the freedom of manoeuvre of the right-of-way yacht.

(c) There are some transitional periods during which rights shift from one yacht to another that need to be provided for.

The right-of-way rules in general apply to yachts racing in open water but, when they approach marks and obstructions, such as shoal water and the shore, in the interests of safety it becomes necessary to make certain exceptions to these rules which will be discussed in due course. In addition, the right of way held by a yacht under one of the basic rules is never absolute; her freedom of manoeuvre is in certain circumstances limited: for example, as already mentioned she may not prevent another yacht from keeping clear.

Finally, the rules recognise that when the right of way shifts abruptly from one yacht to another as, for example, when a yacht establishes an overlap to leeward from clear astern of another, or after a yacht has completed a tack, the erstwhile right-of-way yacht, which is now required to keep clear is entitled to 'ample room and opportunity to keep clear.'

## Minor and Unavoidable Contact

Nobody races boats for long without discovering that collisions and contacts between them do indeed occur from time to time, despite the provisions of the rules. Inevitably, after such incidents the argument revolves round rule 33.2 (Contact Between Yachts Racing) and rule 33.3 (Waiving Rule 33.2).

**Plate 1** To request redress when disabled by a keep-clear yacht, the claimant must have been disabled to an extent which materially affects her speed. A minor bump like this would hardly qualify.          *Alastair Black*

Rule 33.2 stipulates that when there is contact between the hulls, equipment or crew of two yachts, both shall be disqualified or otherwise penalised unless:

either
  (a) one of the yachts retires in acknowledgement of the infringement, or exonerates herself by accepting an alternative penalty, when so prescribed in the sailing instructions,
or
  (b) one or both of the yachts acts in accordance with rule 68 (Protests by Yachts).

Rule 33.3, however, says that a race committee acting under rule 33.2 may waive the requirements of the rule when it is satisfied that the contact was minor and unavoidable. The argument then often turns on what is meant by 'minor and unavoidable.' Case law on this point goes back quite a long way. The earliest recorded appeal known to the author that relates to this point is that of *Marjorie* v *Sheila* and *Nanette* (YRA 1929/7), in which two port-tack close-hauled overlapping International Fourteens were sailing in a light wind, and directly in their course was the paddle-steamer *Fusilier*, which had stopped. Both dinghies tacked to starboard close to *Fusilier's* paddle sponson when she went astern. The surge from her floats caused the windward dinghy to collide with the leeward one when abreast. The YRA (as it then was) exonerated the windward dinghy under the Fundamental Fair Sailing Rule (which was then rule 1).

The object of rule 33.2 is to prevent collusion between two yachts agreeing to ignore a collision and to refrain from protesting, but in light airs and strong tidal streams or currents, particularly when a number of yachts are rounding a mark, two of them may touch without either gaining any advantage. In such circumstances, the rule requires them to protest but, after hearing the evidence of the protests, the protest committee may, in accordance with rule 33.3, waive the requirements of rule 33.2.

There have been several appeals in which neither yacht protested after a 'minor and unavoidable contact' and as a result both were disqualified.

## Rules Revision

In 1961, for the first time in the long history of the sport of yacht racing, all the member national authorities of the International Yacht Racing Union adopted one universal code of racing rules. At the same time, the Permanent Committee of the IYRU decided that these rules should be 'frozen' for a period of four years. The reasons for this decision were twofold:

From long experience it is well known that yachtsmen in general are slow to realise when any changes in the rules are made, and even slower to understand or observe them when they have been made. Some clubs don't even bother to ask the RYA to send them any revised edition of the RYA booklet YR1, the International Racing Rules, which as recognised clubs they are entitled to receive free of charge.

Secondly, any new edition of the rules is timed to come into effect in the first year of a four-year period ending with the next Olympic regatta. This enables potential Olympic competitors to familiarise themselves as early as possible with any rule changes and their effects on tactics and manoeuvres.

It may be of interest to know why and how any changes are made, and to follow the various stages through which such changes pass until they are finally adopted. In initiating any change in the rules, the procedure is described from the point of view of the RYA; other national authorities usually act in a similar manner.

First, it must be stressed that it is not the practice or custom of the IYRU to alter its rules to try to meet or embrace hard or peculiar cases. The saying is, 'hard cases make bad law' and it certainly is a bad thing to alter rules if it can possibly be avoided. It seldom has a good effect and may start a fresh hare or half a dozen fresh hares – take as an example the introduction of alternative penalties to disqualification. Over the years, although the rules have been subjected to a quadrennial revision, there have been very few changes in basic principles, most of the changes have been designed to amplify and clarify the rules, and only a few to cover new developments such as advertising, sponsorship, pumping, ooching and rocking and the wearing of weight jackets.

Rule changes originate in several ways, the commoner ones being appeals against the decisions of protests and requests for redress by race committees and questions from clubs. Throughout this section, the term race committee includes protest committee.

An unsuccessful party to a protest, or one failing to obtain redress, can appeal to the national authority or in USA to the District Appeals Committee, but only on the grounds that the race committee has misapplied the rules. It is a vain endeavour and a waste of time and money to appeal against its findings of fact as, according to rule 74.1 (Finding of Facts), they are final.

It is possible to misinterpret any rule, no matter how carefully it is written, so in such cases, either the race committee, being doubtful about the correctness of its decision, can refer it to the national authority under rule 77.1(c) (Appeals), or the unsuccessful party can appeal under rule 77.1(a) or (b).

When, over a period of time, a number of appeals or questions from clubs relating to the same rule are submitted, and it seems evident that its intention is being quite genuinely misunderstood, in the UK the RYA Racing Rules Committee (RRC) then considers how best to remove any ambiguity and rephrase the rule more precisely.

In addition, there is a regrettable and increasing tendency among some 'sea lawyers' who, having been protested against for a rule infringement and being well aware that they are at fault, will not admit it. At the hearing they will by ingenious argument try to construe the wording of the rules to permit tactics which definitely infringe the rules. They will try to confuse an inexperienced or weak race committee by introducing red herrings and complicating what is essentially a simple rule infringement. Hence, when the arguments advanced by the 'sea lawyers' show a weakness in a rule, that is another reason for amending it.

Since 1961 a valuable relationship has been established between the RRCs of the RYA and the United States Yacht Racing Union (USYRU), and more recently the Canadian Yachting Association. It has become accepted practice before any one of these bodies proceeds with a possible rule amendment, to consult the other two, giving them the details, and the reasons for the proposed change and asking for their views. Quite possibly some further amendments are made until all three bodies are satisfied with the result. This procedure greatly reduces the amount of discussion at the subsequent meeting of the IYRU RRC.

When this stage is reached, the RYA RRC then passes its proposal to the RYA Yacht Racing Divisional Committee for its approval, and when the YRDC agrees with it, the proposal finally goes to the RYA Council for acceptance as a recommended submission to the IYRU RRC. Each proposal is therefore carefully scrutinised by these two bodies, which may in turn may make detailed changes. In its final form it then goes on the agenda for the next meeting of the IYRU RRC, which is circulated to all national authorities at least seven weeks before the RRC meets in London in the following November, for them to brief

their delegates on what attitude they should adopt towards the submission.

The next stage is reached when the IYRU RRC, consisting of a chairman, vice-chairman, sixteen members and two consultants meets to deal with the agenda.

Fortunately for British yachtsmen, all the IYRU meetings are conducted in English, which is the official language used in the text of the racing rules. Difficulties occasionally arise when a foreign member says that he quite understands and fully approves of the purpose of a submission, but objects to its wording because he cannot accurately translate it into his own language and wants to change it and suggests some alternative. Sometimes this is acceptable, but more often than not it fails to convey the precise intended meaning, in which case he must resolve his problem as best he can.

In this connection some years ago a Scots banker, who regularly raced on the Clyde and reckoned he knew the rules well, was posted overseas and in due course started racing again in a local class. During one race he was surprised to be protested against for a rule infringement and was even more surprised to be disqualified. He then wrote to me describing the incident as being between two yachts A and B, without disclosing which of them he was steering and asking for an opinion on which was right. He was told that on the facts given that A was right and he replied saying he was very relieved because he had been steering A. He added that as the national authority under whose jurisdiction he was racing was a member of the IYRU, he assumed that its rules were the same as those under which he had raced in Scotland. He had subsequently read the official translated text and compared it with the relevant English text and found that a vital 'not' had been omitted from the rule, thus reversing its intention.

To prevent hastily-drafted, ill-considered changes being adopted at the last minute, the IYRU Regulation 6.2, Racing Rules reads in part:

'2   During the first three or four years in which the current Racing Rules operate, proposed amendments to the rules of any kind may be submitted and provisionally approved but, except for minor alterations and clarifications, no new principle or major change in principle shall be approved for inclusion in the next revised edition of the rules, unless it has been submitted to the IYRU office in writing and circulated to all National Authorities, at least twelve months before the adoption of such a revised edition of rules.

3   Should a new principle or change in principle be submitted to the IYRU within twelve months before the adoption of a revised edition of the Racing Rules, and when approved by not less than three-quarters of the Racing Rules Committee and by the Permanent Committee, it may be included in the IYRU's next Year Book with the recommendation to National Authorities that they should test it and report on results.'

The usual procedure is that at the end of the first season's experience of a revised edition of the rules, there are few submissions for consideration other than perhaps some errata for correction; at the end of the second season there are more; at the end of the third season there are many more; and at the end of the fourth season, national authorities, realising that the last chance they have of making any significant changes has passed, confine their submissions to amendments of those that have previously been provisionally approved.

In 1960, when the 1961 rules were being drafted, those members of the IYRU RRC who served on the international jury for the Olympic regatta at Naples, before going afloat to watch the racing, met each morning for an hour to study the rules point-by-point and unofficially approve or amend them for the consideration of the full committee in the following November, which procedure greatly expedited their final adoption, and has led to the procedure being repeated at succeeding Olympic regattas.

Finally, when the IYRU RRC has completed its agenda each year, those submissions that have been approved are set out in the minutes of the meeting and are presented by its chairman to the Permanent Committee for its ratification. And so, after the expenditure of a great deal of time, thought and correspondence

by many yachtsmen, a revised edition of the rules is at last ready for printing and distribution – and active use.

So far as the 1981 changes were concerned, the most extensive change was a complete re-write and re-arrangement of the rules of Part VI – Protests, Disqualifications and Appeals, in an attempt to present them in a more logical sequence and to clarify their provisions, including some new definitions.

## Rule Changes

I will now comment on some of the principal changes effected for the period 1981–4, as this may be of interest. The Racing Rules Committee of the IYRU met in London in November 1980. Its main task was to examine some 48 rules submissions (from Canada, France, Great Britain, Holland, the IYRU Class Policy and Organisation Committee, New Zealand and the United States of America) and to decide which of them to recommend to the Permanent Committee for adoption. This meeting ended the four-year rules 'freeze', during which a number of rules amendments were provisionally approved in 1977, 1978 and 1979.

After each submission had been debated and a decision reached, the IYRU then published the approved revised rules and each member country followed suit. In the UK the RYA published their booklet YR/81 *The International Yacht Racing Rules* (including RYA Prescriptions), and these became effective on 1st April 1981. Members of race committees, juries, protest committees, helmsmen and crews should all obtain copies of the revised rules as they are published, and study them carefully; any changes are usually indicated in the text by marginal side lines.

The principal changes affect rule 22.3, Clothing and Equipment; rule 26, now titled Advertisements and Sponsorship; rule 60, Means of Propulsion; and Part VI, Protests, Penalties and Appeals. Appendix 1 (Amateur) no longer includes the International Olympic Committee's rule 26, Eligibility Code, the reasons being, first, that only a very small number of yachtsmen are interested in its provisions and those who may need information on them can obtain it from their national authorities. Secondly, while the IYRU rules are frozen and only printed quadrennially, the IOC rules may be changed at any time.

Appendix 2, previously concerned with pumping, ooching and rocking, now becomes the special Sailboard Racing Rules with many important prescriptions affecting board sailors.

Appendix 2, previously concerned with pumping, ooching and rocking, now becomes the special Sailboard Racing Rules with many important prescriptions affecting board sailors. The main provisions of the original Appendix 2 are incorporated into rule 60, (Means of Propulsion).

Appendix 8 (Terms of Reference of an International Jury and Conditions for its Decisions to be Final) has been revised.

1977 Appendix 9 has been omitted and replaced with excerpts from the International Regulations for Preventing Collisions at Sea, because it was thought that helmsmen should be made aware of the differences between the rules of the IRPCAS and those of the IYRU.

Appendix 11 (Authority and Responsibility of Race Committee and Jury for Rule Enforcement) and Appendix 12 (Organisation of Principal Events) were omitted because the latter was becoming so large, and it was hoped that the IYRU would consider publishing the two appendices in a separate booklet.

A new IYRU Regulation 10, International Judges, specifies the Qualifications and Appointments procedure of International Judges who were appointed to serve during the period 1981–1984.

Dealing, now, with the important changes, rule 22.3, Clothing and Equipment, reads:

(a) (i) Except as permitted by rule 22.3 (b), a competitor shall not wear or

**Plate 2** The rules prohibit the wearing or carrying of clothing or equipment to increase weight. Total weight of clothing and equipment must not exceed 15 kg when soaked with water, unless class rules or the sailing instructions prescribe a lesser or greater weight, in which case such weight shall apply, except that it shall not exceed 20 kg. *Guy Gurney*

carry clothing or equipment for the purpose of increasing his weight.

(ii) Furthermore, the total weight of clothing and equipment worn or carried by a competitor shall not exceed 15 kilograms when soaked with water, and weighed as provided in Appendix 10, (Weighing of Wet Clothing), unless class rules or the sailing instructions prescribe a lesser or greater weight, in which case such weight shall apply, except that it shall not exceed 20 kilograms.

(b) When so prescribed in the class rules, fabric weight jackets and water pockets, compartments or containers in or attached to clothing or equipment shall be permitted, provided that they can be drained or abandoned in less than ten seconds. For the purpose of rule 22.3(a)(ii), the pockets, compartments and containers shall be filled completely with water and included in the total weight.

(c) When a competitor is protested or selected for inspection, he shall produce all containers referred to in rule 22.3(b) which were carried while *racing*.

(d) The organising authority of an offshore event or events for cruiser-racer type yachts may prescribe that rule 22.3(a)(ii) shall not apply to the event or events.

As a general principle, the IYRU prohibits the wearing or carrying of clothing or equipment to increase weight, and their total weight must not exceed 15kg when soaked with water. This is because the IYRU is seriously concerned that so many young competitors have injured their backs through wearing weight jackets and others have drowned. However, it was pointed out that in cold weather the dry clothing of a big competitor, worn solely to keep warm and dry, could exceed 15kg. This was countered to the effect that the latest sailing clothing, specially made to keep warm and dry, would not exceed that limit, although it was agreed that such clothing was expensive and not generally available.

Hence rules 22.3(a)(ii) and 22.3(d) are intended to meet the above circumstances, and rule 22.3(b) enables any particular class association to provide in its class rules that weight jackets can be worn up to a limit of 20kg when

soaked. Of course it could be argued that the whole idea of helping the light chaps to compete on level terms with the heavy ones is misconceived. In practice, both wear weight jackets and the big chaps can carry more weight than the little ones, so the latter are still at a disadvantage. It is also difficult to understand why there is so much sympathy for the little chap in heavy weather, and none for the big chap in light weather.

Rule 26, (Advertisements and Sponsorship) created a long discussion in the IYRU Class Policy and Organisation Committee. Rule 26.1 was slightly changed, re-numbering rules 26.1(a) and (b) as 26.1(a)(i) and (ii), and adding a new rule that reads:

(iii) The yacht's type may be displayed on each side of the hull. The lettering shall not exceed 5cm in height.

This is intended to assist in identifying yachts in a marina or on a trot.

1977 rule 26.2 now becomes 26.1(b) and (c), and 1977 rule 26.3 has been deleted; rule 26.2, Sponsorship, now reads:

(a) A national authority may give consent to a yacht to be supported by a sponsor upon the following terms and conditions:

(i) The name of the sponsor or the name of the sponsor's product or the sponsor's logo shall not be the name of the yacht and shall not be displayed on the hull, sails or equipment except as provided in rule 26.1.

(ii) Within the home waters of that national authority, and when so permitted by another national authority in its waters, the name of the sponsor or the name of the sponsor's product or the sponsor's logo may be displayed on clothing worn by the crew of the yacht provided that rule 26 of the International Olympic Committee is not infringed.

(b) The national authority, in giving consent,

(i) may limit the consent to one event or a series of events.

(ii) may limit the time of its validity.

(iii) shall reserve the right to withdraw such consent, and

(iv) may make such financial arrangements with the sponsor as it sees fit.

**Plate 3**   Read the small print. Rule 25.1(d)(i) requires that '. . . sail numbers shall be above an imaginary line projecting at right angles to the luff from a point one-third of the distance measured from the tack to the head of the sail . . . those on the starboard side being uppermost . . .' K19100 appears to be at fault on both counts.                                                                                                                                                       *Adrian Muttitt*

(c)   When the IYRU or a national authority in conjunction with the IYRU arranges with the sponsor for financial assistance for an international event, the Executive Committee of the IYRU may alter any part or parts of rule 26. A national authority shall request consent from the IYRU at least six months before the event.

The CPOC decided to recommend to the Permanent Committee that rule 26 should not be relaxed to permit the placing of advertisements (names and logos) on yachts' hulls, and rule 26.2 as set out was approved. The object of rule 26.2(c) was to give the IYRU some latitude in regard to such major events as the Whitbread Round-the-World race.

There appears to be some doubt about the identity of the national authority referred to in rules 26.2(a), (b) and (c), although it is intended to be the national authority of the yacht concerned. The difficulty is that under the IYRU constitution, each national authority is autonomous, and one national authority is not bound to accept another's interpretation of rule 26. This could cause serious trouble, for example, in an Admiral's Cup event. Perhaps the organising authority might insert in the notice of the event a statement explaining how it interprets the rule.

The IYRU RRC accepted the general principles of the USYRU submission regarding rule 60, but made some detailed changes in its arrangement and wording. It should not be necessary to reproduce the whole rule here, as the main principle is set out in the second sentence of rule 60.1(b) which reads:

> However, except as provided in rules 60.1(c) and 60.3, no actions, including *tacking* and *gybing*, shall be performed which propel a yacht faster than if the sails, hull and underwater surfaces had been trimmed to best advantage at the time.

The effect of this provision is that although it does not, for example, prohibit roll tacking in such a way that speed is not lost while tacking, it does prohibit it when performed in such a way that after tacking, a yacht is travelling faster than when she began to tack.

In November 1981 the IYRU Executive Committee deleted rule 60.4, (Protests under Rule 60), because it put the onus on the protested yacht, contrary to British jurisprudence in which a defendent is regarded as being innocent until proved guilty.

Some experienced yachtsmen thought that it was inadvisable to revise the 1977 rule 60 at this stage, believing that a number of helmsmen had become familiar with its provisions and knew exactly what was and was not permitted. They felt that race committees were initiating action under the rule, so that it was premature to amend it, but the majority approved the change.

The RYA, in submitting the re-draft of Part VI pointed out that it was a logical extension of the work begun by the IYRU RRC in November 1979 when, among other changes, definitions were introduced and the two rules, 'Hearings' and 'Decisions' were developed and broken down into a number of shorter rules. This work highlighted certain ambiguities, and even contradictions, in Part VI which protest committees over the years had tended to find confusing.

The aims were first to avoid changing the principles on which Part VI is based, secondly to codify procedural rules already accepted in practice and supported by case law, and finally to put the rules in a logical sequence.

Points worth noting are the two new definitions ('rules' and 'protest committee'); the clarification of the position of the race committee or the protest committee when acting against an infringing yacht; the considerable cross-referencing with other rules; and the division into four sections, with almost all the rules titled for identification and guidance.

It is hoped that the rearrangement will make procedures more easily understandable for committees and competitors alike, while remaining flexible enough to satisfy the diversity of situations they must accommodate.

The RYA RRC has for some time been seriously concerned about the number of appeals relating to actions and omissions of juries and protest committees in hearing protests. Close study and observance of the procedural rules in Part VI by those responsible for deciding protests should greatly reduce the work of the RYA RRC and enable justice to be seen to be done.

## Questions

**Q1.1**   What are the fundamental rules?

**Q1.2**   When does a yacht begin to race and become amenable to the racing rules?

**Q1.3**   What are the four basic positional relationships that can exist between two yachts racing, and which yacht has to keep clear in each case?

**Q1.4**   When two yachts touch lightly, and neither gains or loses as a result, are they entitled to agree between themselves to ignore the incident?

# 2 Altering Course

It may be of interest to point out that, although the racing rules were first codified in the UK in 1875 by the Yacht Racing Association (now the Royal Yachting Association), there was no rule relating to altering course until one was introduced in 1908, when the International Yacht Racing Union adopted its own code of rules for use in European waters, based on the YRA rules then in force.

This new rule resulted from the classic case of *Tramontana* v *Triphon* (YRA 1904/9). These two yachts were running on starboard tack with spinnakers set for a leeward starboard-hand mark. *Tramontana* was leading by about 50 yards with *Triphon* dead astern (Fig. 1a). Their normal course after luffing round the mark was close-hauled on the same starboard

tack. However, on rounding the mark, *Tramontana*, to avoid a calm patch in her normal course, tacked short to port, becoming close-hauled, on port tack, right under *Triphon's* bows. At that time YRA rule 28 (Yachts Meeting) stated that:

> A yacht which is running free shall keep out of the way of a yacht which is close-hauled.

*Triphon* bore away all she could to avoid a collision until she was running by the lee, then gybed and her boom hit *Tramontana*.

*Triphon* claimed that *Tramontana* had caused a foul and, as no other rule applied, she should be disqualified under rule 1 – now the Fundamental Fair Sailing rule. *Tramontana* argued that under rule 28 it was *Triphon's* duty to keep clear in any circumstances. The race committee disqualified *Triphon*, but referred its decision to the YRA, which ruled that under rule 1 *Tramontana* had no right to tack short under *Triphon's* bows so as to risk a collision, and disqualified *Tramontana*. This case led to the framing of 1908 IYRU rule 30(k) (Altering Course), which read:

> When by any of the above clauses (of rule 30) one yacht has to keep out of the way of another, the latter (subject to clause (b)) shall not alter course so as to prevent her doing so.

Clause (b) was the luffing clause, now rule 38.1 (Luffing Rights).

YRA rule 28 ceased to apply in 1959. Under the present rules, *Triphon* would hold right of way under rule 36 (Opposite Tacks – Basic Rule), but the situation can still arise in the mirror image of Fig. 1a as shown in Fig. 1b.

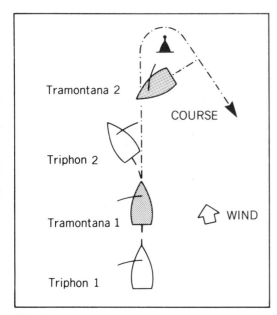

**Fig. 1a**

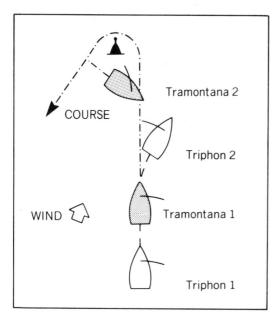

**Fig. 1b**

Here, if *Tramontana* (2) were allowed to tack short to starboard round the mark, and *Triphon* (2), having been on port tack, bore away and gybed on to starboard, *Triphon* would then rank as the windward yacht under rule 37.1 and would be bound to keep clear of *Tramontana* (2). The present rule 35 given below prohibits *Tramontana* from precipitating such an unexpected and dangerous situation. Let us therefore examine some of the situations that are governed by rule 35, which reads as follows:

**35  Limitations on Altering Course**

> When one yacht is required to keep clear of another, the right-of-way yacht shall not so alter course as to prevent the other yacht from keeping clear, or so as to obstruct her while she is keeping clear, except:
>
> (a)   to the extent permitted by rule 38.1 (Same Tack, Luffing and Sailing above a Proper Course after Starting), and
> (b)   when assuming a *proper course*:
>       either
>       (i)    to *start*, unless subject to rule 40 (Same Tack, Luffing before Starting), or to the second part of rule 44.1(b) (Returning to Start).
>       or
>       (ii)   when rounding a *mark*.

## Obstruction

The first point to stress is that rule 35 applies only to the yacht holding right of way under any rule in Part IV. It issues a command to her by saying in effect 'When you hold right of way - when your opponent must keep clear of you - do not alter course in such a manner as will prevent her from keeping clear, or obstruct her while she is doing so. It is no good saying that you have right of way and will sail just where you jolly well please; you have to give her a fair chance to keep clear.'

This does not mean that the right-of-way yacht cannot alter course at all; she can do so, but subject always to rule 35. The right-of-way rules are specifically framed to ensure safety and equity, and this is a good example of that spirit in action.

The first situation is somewhat similar to that described in the case of *Tramontana* v *Triphon*. Looking a Fig. 2(A), WP is on port tack with her spinnaker set, storming downwind with everything pulling, and is meeting LP close-hauled on port tack. WP is an unhandy craft compared with the close-hauled yacht but, as the windward yacht under rule 37.1 (Same Tack – Basic Rule), she must keep clear of the leeward yacht LP. It would be dangerous and bad seamanship for WP to luff

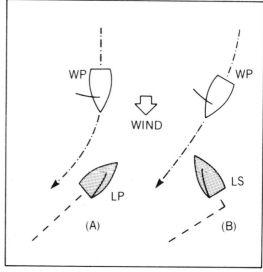

**Fig. 2**

and try to cross ahead of LP, so her correct avoiding action would be to bear away dead before the wind, or even by the lee, to pass astern of LP, but she will only have to do so for a few moments, then she will be clear. When WP alters course, LP becomes bound by rule 35 not to alter her course so as to prevent WP from keeping clear. She must not tack spitefully to starboard, as shown at LS in Fig. 2(B), and claim that WP must still keep clear under the Opposite Tacks – Basic rule 36. That would be a clear infringement of rule 35.

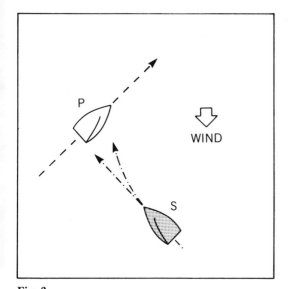

**Fig. 3**

The second situation is shown in Fig. 3, where P, close-hauled on port tack, will cross clear ahead of S, close-hauled on starboard tack, provided that S holds her course and that there is no sudden wind shift. In the first edition of Paul Elvström's book on the rules, the author failed to realise the limitations imposed by rule 35. Apparently relying on rule 36, he said that S had the right to luff head to wind if she pleased, because she would technically be on a tack and, if she were prevented from luffing by the presence of P, then P was wrong. This interpretation was wrong, and it unfortunately misled race committees and helmsmen, causing a number of incorrect decisions on protests, and the lodging of subsequent appeals.

It was wrong for three reasons. First, rule 35 clearly prohibits S from altering course, that is luffing, so as to prevent P from keeping clear or so as to obstruct her while she was keeping clear. Secondly, in the case of the Salcombe Yacht Club (RYA 1968/2, IYRU Case 36), the question was asked whether rule 36 over-rode rule 35 in such a way as to entitle S to steer a course deliberately to hit P by luffing or bearing away. The answer was 'No', because rule 35 is in Section B of Part IV and always applies, except when over-ridden by a rule in Section C. And thirdly, as P and S were on opposite tacks, S had no right to luff head to wind as she pleased, because rule 38.1, mentioned in rule 35(a), is a same-tack rule and therefore did not apply. That misinterpretation was corrected in subsequent editions, but its effect persisted for a long time.

The third situation is shown in Fig. 4. Boat P, close-hauled on port tack, is bound by rule 36 to keep clear of S. If P alters course to keep clear by bearing away to pass astern of S as shown, S must not alter course by bearing away as shown in the dotted outline. That too is a clear infringement of rule 35.

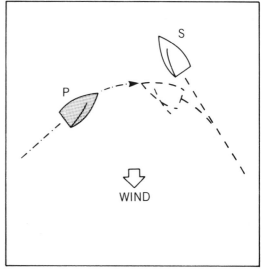

**Fig. 4**

The fourth situation is shown in Fig. 5 and illustrates the case of *Thalassa* v *Aldebaran* (RYA 1965/6; IYRU Case 23). P was

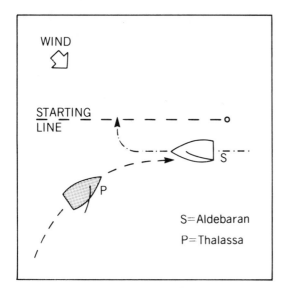

**Fig. 5**

approaching the starting line on port tack. S, on starboard tack, was sailing close to, and on the pre-start side of, the starting line. P bore away to pass astern of S. At the same time, S tacked to port to fetch the first mark, and the swing of her stern caused P to bear away even more. The RYA ruled that S's tack constituted a clear infringement of rules 35 and 41.1 (Changing Tacks – Tacking and Gybing), and disqualified her.

What is meant by the word 'obstruct'? In the case of the Barnt Green Sailing Club (RYA 1972/2), which is similar to the preceding case, it is defined as follows:

> Obstruct, in the context of rule 35, means putting the give-way yacht at a disadvantage greater than that which she would have suffered in complying with her obligations if the right-of-way yacht had held her course.

## Illegal Luffing

It is important to realise that rule 35(a) states that luffing, as defined in rule 38.1, by a leeward yacht or a yacht clear ahead does not infringe rule 35, but the case of *Tornado* v *Chaos* (RYA 1965/7) demonstrates that an illegal luff does infringe that rule (Fig. 6). S and P were

running towards the leeward mark on opposite tacks, about three-quarters of a length apart, with S slightly ahead. S luffed suddenly, at least 10 degrees, without any warning or hail, and four seconds later hit P.

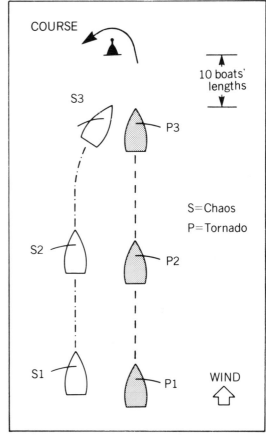

**Fig. 6**

P knew that S had right of way, but did not foresee that such an alteration of course might be made. S was disqualified under rule 34.1 (Hailing), and she appealed, maintaining that it was not unforeseen alteration of course and that rule 34 could not apply. Her appeal was upheld to the extent that P was disqualified as well as S! The RYA's decision stated that, as the yachts were on opposite tacks, rule 38.1 did not apply and S was prohibited from making a sudden luff. The fact that P and S sailed abreast for some distance did not relieve P of her obligation under rule 36 (Opposite Tracks – Basic Rule) to keep clear of S at all times.

Under rule 32 (Avoiding Collisions), the right-of-way yacht, S, was bound to try to avoid collision. In fact, her sudden alteration of course caused one.

'Prior to the alteration of course, both yachts were running clear of each other. The moment S luffed suddenly, P had to take immediate action to keep clear. In this instance, the violence of the luff prevented P from keeping clear, contrary to rule 35 (Limitations on Altering Course). P is disqualified under rule 36. S is disqualified under rules 32 and 35.'

The USSR Yacht Racing Federation submitted a somewhat similar situation (IYRU Case 35) and shown in Fig. 7. W and L were running on port tack abreast, about three to five metres apart for about ten minutes. W then gybed, thus becoming S, without infringing rule 41.1 (Changing Tacks – Tacking or Gybing), and L, now P, held her course; both yachts continued to sail parallel courses. About two minutes after S had gybed, she hailed P and began to luff; the yachts touched. The question asked was 'Did S hold right of way under rule 36, or did rule 35 apply?'

In its answer, the IYRU said: 'S, having completed her gybe in accordance with rule 41.1, was the starboard-tack right-of-way yacht under rule 36, and P, as the port-tack yacht, was bound to keep clear. In this situation rule 38.1 did not apply, so S had no right to luff 'as she pleased'. Nevertheless, she was not bound to hold her course, and could alter it by luffing in such a way that she did not infringe rule 35.'

## Wind Shift

In discussing the situation shown in Fig. 3, it was said that P is able to cross clear ahead of S, provided that S holds her course and that 'there is no *sudden* wind shift.'

In the case of *Flamingo* v *Gadfly*; *Gadfly* v *Flamingo* (RYA 1971/6; IYRU Case 52), there was a sudden substantial wind shift (Fig. 8). At position 1, both yachts were close-hauled on opposite tacks and P was crossing clear ahead of S. The wind veered through about 45 degrees, heading P and freeing S, and both yachts altered course to conform to the new wind direction, as in position 2.

S did not sail above her close-hauled course, and had to bear away to avoid a collision with P. S protested against P under rule 36, and P counter-protested under rule 35. P alleged that the wind shift was abnormally large; that after the wind shift it was impossible for her to keep clear – a fact that S did not dispute – and that P could not tack without infringing rule 41.1. P further asserted that S should not so alter course with the wind shift as to prevent P from keeping clear, even if this required S, the right-of-way yacht, to sail below her proper close-hauled course.

The race committee disqualified P under rule 36, on the grounds that she should not have crossed S with so little margin of safety

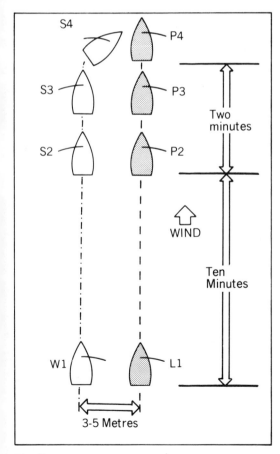

**Fig. 7**

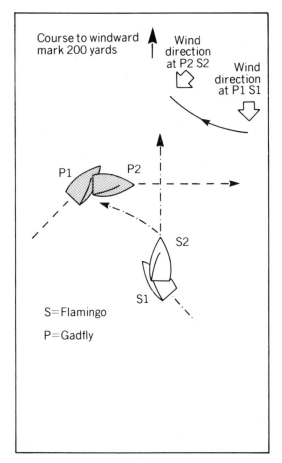

**Fig. 8**

that, in the event of a wind shift at the moment of or immediately after her crossing, P would be unable to keep clear of S. The decision was referred to the RYA under rule 77.1(c) (Appeals).

The RYA did not uphold P's disqualification, and P's protest under rule 35 was dismissed for the following reasons: 'It was agreed that, at position P1S1, P was crossing clear ahead of S, that is, had the wind not shifted, P was keeping clear. S, being the right-of-way yacht, was entitled to take advantage of the wind shift, but she was also bound by rule 35 not to alter course so as to prevent P from keeping clear. As S altered course again to avoid a collision with P, she did not infringe rule 35. Neither yacht infringed any rule.'

Note that the 1961 rule 34 (Misleading or Baulking) reads:

2   A yacht is not misleading or baulking another if she alters course by luffing or bearing away to conform to a change in the strength or direction of the wind.

But this provision was deleted from 1969 rule 34 (Limitations on the Right-of-Way Yacht to Alter Course), partly because those terms – misleading and baulking – were also deleted, and partly because the relaxation was judged to be undesirable.

Turning now to the exceptions to rule 35, rule 35(a) merely makes it clear that a luff under rule 38.1 is permissible. The proviso in rule 35(b)(i) was introduced in 1973 to cover the situation shown in Fig. 9. At position 1, S is reaching on starboard tack on the pre-start side of the starting line just before the starting signal is made, while P is on a close-hauled port-tack course to start which, if S holds her course, will enable P to cross and clear S.

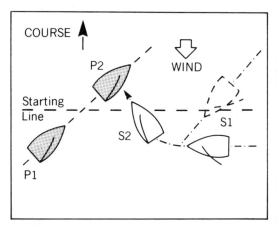

**Fig. 9**

The question was: 'If, at the starting signal, S luffs to a close-hauled 'proper' course, as shown at position 2, does she infringe rule 35 by preventing P from keeping clear?' Rule 35(b)(i) makes it evident that the answer is 'No', S is entitled to assume a proper course and P must anticipate that S will do so. This rule also ensures that when S is on the course side of the starting line, as shown in the dotted outline – assuming that the Round the Ends starting rule in rule 51.1(c) does not apply – and dips back to the pre-start side of the starting line, she is bound by rule 44.1(b) to allow P, who is starting correctly, 'room and opportunity to keep clear'.

## Rounding a Mark

Rule 35(b)(ii) was introduced in 1977 and covers the situation shown in Fig. 10, in which two yachts approach a mark on opposite tacks. In the case of *Mistral* v *Endeavour* (YRA 1947/2), *Mistral*, P, reached the mark clear ahead of *Endeavour*, S. P tacked to round the mark onto a port-tack reach. Owing to the set of the tide, she made a poor rounding and her speed over the ground was slow. S approached the mark on starboard tack. P claimed that had S held her course, she would have passed clear astern of P. Instead, S luffed and she struck P's starboard quarter. P protested under what is now rule 35, and S counter-protested under rule 36.

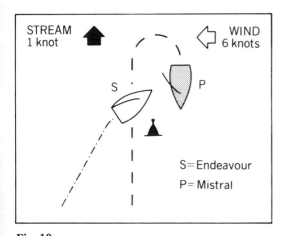

STREAM
1 knot

WIND
6 knots

S = Endeavour

P = Mistral

**Fig. 10**

The race committee found that at no time did S alter course to prevent P taking avoiding action; P was on port tack and it was her duty to keep clear of S. P was disqualified under rule 36.

P appealed and argued that rule 36 imposed a duty on her to keep clear, and that rule 35 imposed a duty on S not to prevent her from doing so. P claimed that, having tacked, she could fulfil her duty either by going under S's

stern or by crossing ahead of her, provided that she, P, could do so without making S alter course or colliding with her. P maintained that there was no duty on her to anticipate either S's luffing or bearing away – P had to keep clear of where S was, not where she might be. P had to be prepared for S altering course, but was entitled to assume that S would not alter course in such a way as to prevent P from keeping clear.

P asserted that for S to alter course in such a way that P could not comply with rule 36 was an infringement of rule 35. The fact that P could easily have avoided S by taking certain action before S luffed was irrelevant, claimed P, because until S's luff brought about a probability of collision, there was no obligation on P to alter course. The YRA dismissed P's appeal.

The object of rule 35(b)(ii) is to make it clear that, when rounding a mark, the right-of-way yacht, S, is entitled to assume a proper course for precisely the same reasons as she is allowed to assume a proper course to start. P must anticipate that S will round the mark, and P must give S room to do so.

## Questions

**Q2.1** Under which circumstances may a right-of-way yacht alter course in such a way that she might prevent the give-way yacht from keeping clear, or obstruct her while she is trying to keep clear?

**Q2.2** When a yacht tacks or gybes into a position which will give her right of way over another yacht on a tack, she must do so far enough away so that the latter can keep clear without having to alter course until after the tack or gybe has been completed. But who has to show that the tack or gybe was or was not completed in time – the yacht tacking or the one trying to keep clear?

**Q2.3** Can a right-of-way yacht alter course regardless of the proximity of a give-way yacht?

**Q2.4** Can a close-hauled starboard tack yacht take advantage of a freeing windshift, when a close-hauled port-tack yacht is crossing ahead of her?

**Q2.5** Can a close-hauled starboard-tack yacht luff head to wind and try to hit a close-hauled port-tack yacht that will cross clear ahead of her if the starboard-tack yacht holds her course?

**Q2.6** What, in the context of rule 35, is meant by the term 'obstruct'?

# 3 Opposite Tacks

## Basic Rule

With regard to the first basic positional relationship, the Opposite Tacks – Basic Rule 36 simply says:

> A *port-tack* yacht shall keep clear of a *starboard-tack* yacht.

By definition:

A yacht is *on a tack* except when she is *tacking* or *gybing*. A yacht is on the *tack* (*starboard* or *port*) corresponding to her *windward* side.

The starboard side of a yacht is the right-hand side when looking towards her bows; the port side is the left-hand side.

In Fig. 11, any one of the port-tack yachts P1–P4 must keep clear of any one of the starboard-tack yachts S1–S4, except in the following four special situations.

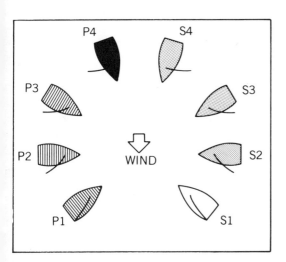

**Fig. 11**

1. When, as shown in Fig. 12, the starboard-tack yacht, S1, either has made a premature start and is returning to start, or she is on the course side of the starting line when the starting signal is made and is working into position to start; she must in either case keep clear of all yachts which are starting or have started correctly, until she is wholly on the pre-start side of the starting line (rule 44.1(a) (Returning to Start). Even then, when she is wholly on the pre-start side of the starting line and thereby newly acquires starboard-tack rights over P5, as shown at S2P5, S2 must allow P5 'ample room and opportunity to keep clear' (rule 44.1(b)).

2. When, after starting and clearing the starting line, the port-tack yacht, P in Fig. 13, has established an inside overlap in proper time on the starboard-tack yacht S, and when both are running to a starboard-hand mark or an obstruction, rule 42.1(a) (Rounding or Passing Marks and Obstructions) over-rides the Opposite Tacks—Basic Rule 36, and the outside yacht S must give the yacht overlapping her on the inside, P, room to round or pass the mark or obstruction.

3. When two overlapping yachts on opposite tacks, S and P in Fig. 14, are running to a port-hand leeward mark, round which S will have to gybe in order most directly to assume a proper course to the next mark, S must gybe as soon as she has room to do so. In such conditions, rule 42.1(b) over-rides rule 36. S therefore cannot claim starboard-tack rights over P and sail her past the mark.

4. When a yacht, S1 in Fig. 15, has touched a mark and either is about to exonerate her-

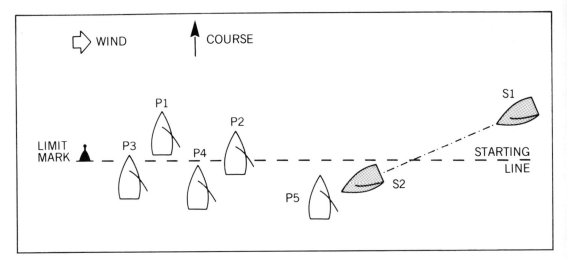

**Fig. 12**

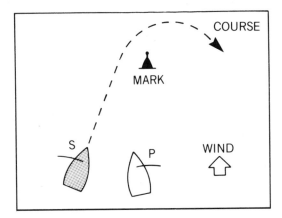

**Fig. 13**

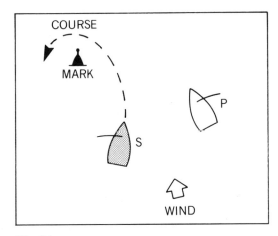

**Fig. 14**

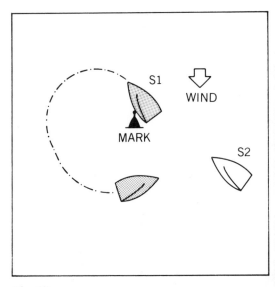

**Fig. 15**

self or is exonerating herself by re-rounding it, she must keep clear of S2 and all other yachts which are about to round or pass the mark correctly, until she has cleared it and is on a proper course to the next mark—rule 45.1 (Re-rounding after Touching a Mark).

## Right of Way Transfer

Incidents involving port-tack and starboard-tack yachts occur on virtually every beat of every race, and the successful helmsman must know how to turn an apparently disadvantageous port-tack approach into a position of distinct advantage when faced with a right-of-way starboard-tack yacht; but at the same time he treads a very fine line in staying within the rules.

**Onus of Proof**
For example, port-tack yacht P tacks dead ahead of starboard-tack yacht S. Now P must complete her tack onto starboard at such a distance that S can hold her course until P has completed her tack and S then has room to keep clear, either by luffing or by bearing away. Initially, under the Opposite Tacks—Basic rule 36, S has right of way over P. Then, provided that in tacking P observes rule 41.2 (which says that a yacht must not tack into a right-of-way position without leaving sufficient room for the other yacht to keep clear), the right-of-way is transferred to her, as she is now the yacht clear ahead which, under rule 37.2 (Same Tack—Basic Rules), requires S, now the yacht clear astern, to keep clear. However, a clause of rule 41 (Tacking and Gybing) applies to the whole manoeuvre and puts the onus of proof onto the tacking yacht. This clause reads:

> A yacht which *tacks* or *gybes* has the onus of satisfying the race committee that she completed her *tack* or *gybe* in accordance with rule 41.2.

And it is this onus of proof that can cause so many problems for protest committees and the parties involved.

Owing to a change in relationship between two yachts, it is a general principle that, when the right of way is transferred from one yacht to the other, the yacht that originally held right of way is under no obligation to anticipate any such change in relationship; and also that the yacht which newly acquires right of way shall allow the other yacht ample room and opportunity to keep clear. Rules 37.3, 41.1, 42.3 and 44.2 refer, but this principle does not apply to rule 38 (Same Tack—Luffing and Sailing above a Proper Course after Starting).

This onus is placed on P because, in tacking, she initiates a new situation for which she alone is responsible and from which she derives a great advantage. If P has room to complete her tack to starboard, she could also hold her course and cross clear ahead of S, and so avoid interfering with S.

Rule 41.3 is excellent in that it gives much guidance to protest committees. In fact, it could be said that this principle is so useful that, although no positive indication is given in the rules that it should be a general one, it is in practice (and often quite rightly) applied completely out of context—i.e. when neither of the yachts involved is actually tacking or gybing.

The only other rules that specify an onus of satisfying the race committee are rules 42.3(d), 42.3(e) and 43.2(b)(iii). In addition to these rules, the RYA decided in the case of *Bosun No. 56* v *Bosun No. 58* (RYA 1973/3) that the onus lies on the windward yacht claiming Mast Abeam, under rule 38.4, Hailing to Stop or Prevent a Luff.

It has apparently become standard practice among some protest committees to adopt a procedure of first deciding which yacht is in the wrong, and then putting the onus on her to prove that she was right and, if she cannot, disqualifying her. This, of course, makes total nonsense of justice and the rules, and works only sometimes, depending on which rules it is applied to. The favourite is rule 36; when a collision has occurred, the port-tack yacht is presumed wrong unless she can satisfy the protest committee that she was not.

It is to be hoped that this kind of procedure for conducting a protest hearing is followed only by very few protest committees. The correct procedure is for each party to a protest at the hearing to give his evidence, perhaps supported by witnesses, when each can question the accuracy of the other's statement. When all the evidence has been heard, each party is entitled to make a final statement of his case, including any application or interpretation of the rules to the incident as he sees it. This is the time for him to try to refute any statements the other party may have made with which he disagrees. The atmosphere at a

**Plate 4**    *Jan Pot* ploughs into *Griffin III* at the start of a race during Cowes Week one year.    *Jonathan Eastland*

protest hearing could often be much more pleasant, and the task of the protest committee much simpler, if both parties would follow this procedure.

When this stage of the proceeding has been reached, and only then, the parties should be asked to withdraw while the protest committee finds the facts. It is often helpful for the committee to decide from those facts which yacht originally was required to keep clear, a point that is sometimes overlooked, and to bear in mind where the onus, if any, lies.

In the case of *Sinnes* v *Lord Osis* (RYA 1967/7; IYRU Case 77), the RYA ruled:

When two yachts collide, there must have been an infringement of a rule and the protest committee must, under rule 71 (Decisions), on a protest arising from the incident find the relevant facts and give a decision on them. When there is a protest arising from an incident that did not involve a collision, it is open to the protest committee, in the face of lack of evidence or of conflicting evidence, to dismiss the protest on the grounds that it is not satisfied that there has been an infringement of any rule.

It is a fundamental principle of English jurisprudence that a person charged with an offence is considered to be innocent until proved guilty. Hence, under the International Yacht Racing Union's jurisprudence, it is for the protestor to convince the protest committee that his allegation is true, rather than for the protestee to satisfy the committee that he did not infringe a rule and, in any case of doubt, that doubt should be resolved in his favour, unless a collision occurred or the rules place an onus upon him.

Note that neither the basic opposite-tacks rule nor the basic same-tack rule contains an onus clause. When the IYRU Racing Rules Committee was revising the 1973 rules, it rejected a proposal that rule 36 should contain such a clause. The RRC concluded that a

**Plate 5** A dramatic port-and-starboard collision at the start of the 1979 Mini-Transat. Apart from avoiding the encounter completely, when faced with the inevitable, each yacht should avoid presenting her beam to the other's bow. In the Mini-Transat collision, both yachts should have luffed. In the Cowes Week meeting, *Jan Pot* should have borne away, while *Griffin* luffed – again to avoid crossing ahead. Note that rule 15 of the International Regulations for Preventing Collisions at Sea says, in part: '... and shall, if the circumstances of the case admit, avoid crossing ahead of the other vessel.'
*Flagpic*

protest committee should decide a case on the facts it found. However, Appeal No 32 of the North American Yacht Racing Union (now the United States Yacht Racing Union) dated 19th October 1949, states:

When there is reasonable doubt as to the ability of the port-tack yacht to cross ahead of a starboard-tack yacht, the starboard-tack yacht is entitled to bear away and protest, and need for adequate evidence rests on the obligated port-tack yacht to support her claim that she would have cleared the starboard-tack yacht.

The RYA cited this case with approval in reply to a question from the Queensland Yachting Association (1959/17), and in the case of *F1120* v *F11* (RYA 1973/1). See also *Alana II* v *Magic*, CYA 5/1979, IYRU Case 113.

## Collision Course

Let us now consider what may happen on a windward leg when two close-hauled yachts are approaching one another on collision courses. First, in the case of the Karachi YC v *Alouette* and *Zephyrus* (RYA 1953/10), the council commented that 'it is not a custom of the sea to neglect to keep a proper look-out at all times', and in the case of *Hellhound* v *Hare* (RYA 1971/4; IYRU Case 51), it ruled:

The rules of Part IV are specifically framed to avoid collision. All yachts, whether or not holding right of way, are at all times bound to keep a good look-out.

Secondly, although not required by the rules, when S sees P approaching on a collision course, it is sporting and seamanlike for S to hail 'Starboard!' to ensure that P is aware of S's proximity, and for P to acknowledge the hail by a hand signal or by replying 'Hold your course', or words to that effect.

Thirdly, when P does not immediately begin to alter course, it does not necessarily follow that she will not do so shortly. Among experienced helmsmen who can rely on their opponents strictly observing the rules, it is normal practice for P to hold her course without interfering with S, until she can accurately judge the distance and position at which she will, to her best advantage, either tack and lee-bow S, or bear away the minimum amount to clear her stern with the least possible loss of weather gage. Meanwhile S holds her course, knowing that P will keep clear.

However, should it become obvious to S that if she holds her course a collision resulting in serious damage is imminent, she becomes bound by rule 32 (Avoiding Collisions) to make a reasonable attempt to avoid the collision, otherwise she risks disqualification as well as P. In the case of *Hellhound* v *Hare*, because the right-of-way yacht S made no attempt to avoid a collision in time for such action to be effective, and because serious damage resulted, S was disqualified under rule 32. In fact, as a result of the collision the two yachts, a Soling and a 505, were locked together, P (the 505) being firmly impaled on S's bow which had crashed through the hull just abaft the mast, gone through the side buoyancy tank, and finished up short of the centreboard case.

From a practical point of view, in trying to avoid a collision both yachts must alter course in the same way. When S judges that, if she holds her course she will ram P amidships or farther forward, both yachts must luff. But if S will ram P aft of amidships, both yachts must bear away sharply.

Now we come to difficult ground because to a novice steering S, assuming that P intends to keep clear, the close proximity of P may appear to be a terrifyingly dangerous situation calling for immediate avoiding action when, in fact, no such action is needed. Here, if S protests, P will have to convince the protest committee that she was well aware of S's proximity, and was holding her course until she could accurately judge when she could tack or bear away, and that there was no likelihood of there being a collision. This is where, if justice is to be done, an experienced protest committee is essential, preferably familiar with the characteristics of the yachts in the class concerned, to come to the right conclusion.

An equally difficult problem faces a protest committee when hearing a protest in which P insists that she was quite confident that she could safely cross ahead of S, but S is unscrupulous and alters course and protests, claiming that had she not done so, there would have been a collision. The only practical answer to offer to P, is not to cross ahead of S if she is likely to cut it rather fine, unless she knows that S's helmsman is a true sportsman.

## Questions

**Q3.1**  PL has established a leeward overlap on PW from clear astern and, as leeward yacht, holds right of way over PW. PW can cross ahead of S coming in on starboard tack, but PL cannot cross her. PL could bear away and pass under the stern of S, but she does not want to lose so much ground. Is PL bound by rule 41.2 (Changing Tacks—Tacking and Gybing) which prevents her tacking into PW?

**Q3.2**  SW can safely pass into the bay ahead, but SL cannot and hails her for room to tack and clear the obstruction ahead of her. What should SW do?

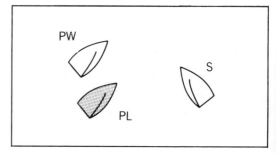

**Fig. Q3.2**

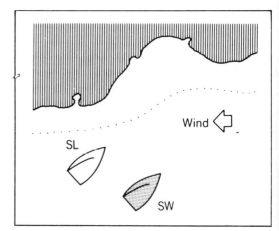

**Fig. Q3.1**

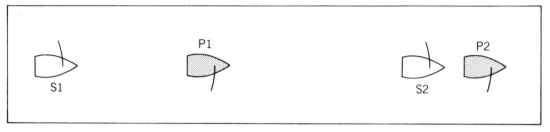

**Fig. Q3.3**

**Q3.3**  Which has right of way between S and P?

**Q3.4**  Local geographical features sometimes cause some rules to be more often involved in protests than others. The River Yealm in Devon, UK, has high hills which slope steeply down to the river and they prompted this and the next question from the local club. A port-gybe Enterprise dinghy was involved with a starboard-gybe Laser. The protest committee decided that the boats were on converging courses but, if they had been on parallel courses, could the Laser have sailed by the lee to enforce her position, rather than being windward boat on the same tack?

**Q3.5**  In a close-hauled opposite-tack situation, can the starboard-tack yacht alter course to maintain a steady close-hauled course (there are quite large wind shifts in some parts of the creek)?

**Q3.6**  A premature starter has responded to a recall and is returning on starboard tack to start correctly. What rights has she over a port-tack yacht that is starting or has started correctly?

**Q3.7**  Having wholly returned to the pre-start side of the line, is the premature starter of Q3.6 subject to any further limitations?

**Q3.8**  Are there any other exceptions to rule 36 (Opposite Tacks—Basic Rule)? If so, name them.

**Q3.9**  At what distance must a port-tack yacht (P) complete her tack to starboard dead ahead of a starboard-tack yacht (S) which is on a tack, so as not to infringe rule 41 (Tacking and Gybing)?

**Q3.10**  When, owing to a change in relationship between two yachts, the right of way is transferred from one yacht to the other, what general principles apply?

# 4 Same Tack-Basic Rules

Excluding the third and fourth basic positional relationships mentioned on page 2, if two yachts at close quarters are not on opposite tacks, they must be on the same tack, in which case rule 37 (Same Tack—Basic Rules) will apply. Note that this rule is sub-titled 37.1 When Overlapped, 37.2 When not Overlapped, and 37.3 Transitional.

**Plate 6** Mirror 60998 has established a windward overlap on 58040, because the definition says that yachts overlap when neither is clear astern; which, in turn, is defined as when one yacht's hull and equipment in normal position are abaft an imaginary line projected abeam from the aftermost point of the other's hull and equipment in normal position. Here, 60998's spinnaker is not clear astern of 58040's rudder.     *Arthur Sidey*

# Overlap

What is meant by the term 'overlap' ? By definition:

A yacht is *clear astern* of another when her hull and equipment in normal position are abaft an imaginary line projected abeam from the aftermost point of the other's hull and equipment in normal position. The other is *clear ahead*. The yachts *overlap* when neither is *clear astern*; or when, although one is *clear astern*, an intervening yacht *overlaps* both of them. The terms *clear astern*, *clear ahead* and *overlap* apply to yachts on opposite *tacks* only when they are subject to rule 42 (Rounding or Passing Marks and Obstructions).

In Fig. 16, as L is not abaft W's stern line, neither is clear astern of the other, so they overlap. As B is abaft the stern lines of both L and W, B ranks as a yacht clear astern of both the others.

## Windward and Leeward

Rule 37.1 reads:

> When overlapped a *windward yacht* shall keep clear of a *leeward yacht*.

What is a windward yacht and what is a leeward yacht?

According to the definition of leeward and windward:

The *leeward* side of a yacht is that on which she is, or, when head to wind, was, carrying her mainsail. The opposite side is the *windward* side. When neither of two yachts on the same *tack* is *clear astern*, the one on the leeward side of the other is the *leeward yacht*. The other is the *windward yacht*.

Hence, in Fig. 16, L ranks as the leeward yacht, and W ranks as the windward yacht, and rule 37.1 requires W to keep clear of L. As B is abaft the stern lines of both L and W, B ranks as a yacht clear astern of both.

## Intervening

What is meant by the term 'an intervening yacht'? It will be seen in Fig. 17(a) that, by definition, M (middle or intervening yacht) overlaps L, and W overlaps M. Therefore, as M is between L and W, she ranks as an intervening yacht and L and W also overlap. However, in Fig. 17(b), although W overlaps L, and BL overlaps W, W is not between them, so L and BL do not overlap. This important distinction is not always understood.

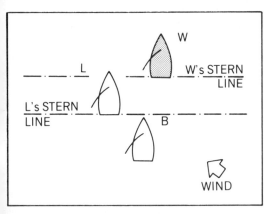

**Fig. 16**

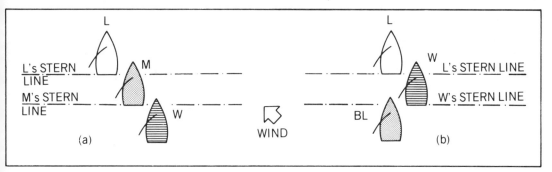

**Fig. 17**

**Plate 7**   *Definition.* The yachts overlap when neither is clear astern; or when, although one is clear astern, an intervening yacht overlaps both of them.

## No Overlap

Rule 37.2 says:

> When not overlapped a yacht *clear astern* shall keep clear of a yacht *clear ahead*.

This partly supports the principle laid down in rule 13(a) of the International Regulations for Preventing Collisions at Sea, which states that any vessel overtaking any other shall keep out of the way of the vessel being overtaken—but only to the extent that the IYRU rule applies to yachts on the same tack; a starboard-tack yacht, S, clear astern of a port-tack yacht, P, and running up on P, has right of way under rule 36.

There is here, therefore, a most important difference between the yacht racing rules and the International Regulations for Preventing Collisions at Sea which govern the behaviour of all vessels at sea, and it is important for the racing helmsman always to remember that he is bound by the latter when he meets another vessel which is not herself racing. Under IRPCAS a racing yacht or dinghy, running on starboard gybe and coming up from a direction more than 22½ degrees aft of the beam (the official overtaking zone) of a yacht or dinghy on port gybe which is not racing, would be required to keep clear, even though the racing yacht is on starboard and the other on port; but she would have right of way if the other were racing, either in her class or in another class. Note that the sailing instructions of any race which is expected to continue after sunset usually prescribe that the International Regulations for Preventing Collisions at Sea shall apply to yachts still racing after dark.

**Plate 8**    Laser 7355 is clear astern of 19539, without any doubt.                    *William Rowntree*

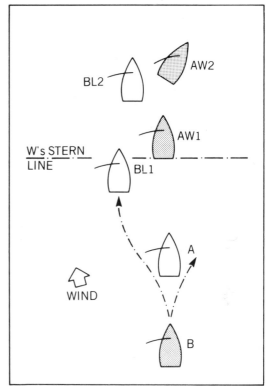

**Fig. 18**

## Establishing a Leeward Overlap

Going back to the racing rules, when B, the yacht clear astern in Fig. 18, is sailing in the wake of A, the yacht clear ahead, and runs up on her, rule 37.2 requires B to keep clear of A, and B has the option of trying to pass either to leeward or to windward of A. When B elects to try to pass to leeward and establishes an overlap on A, B is governed by rule 37.3, which reads:

Transitional: A yacht which establishes an *overlap* to *leeward* from *clear astern* shall allow the *windward yacht* ample room and opportunity to keep clear.

There are some limitations on the right-of-way yacht's freedom of manoeuvre, and there are some transitional periods during which rights shift from one yacht to another for which provision needs to be made, and rule 37.3 is an example.

## Room to Keep Clear

When BL establishes her overlap on AW (BL1/AW1 in Fig. 18), BL must take care to allow AW 'ample room and opportunity to keep clear.' BL must not establish her overlap so close to AW that if, for example, AW luffs—head to wind if she pleases—to fulfil her newly acquired obligation to keep clear, her stern swings towards BL and hits her; or if, when AW trims her mainsheet, her boom touches BL's forestay or weather shroud, this indicates that BL has not given AW 'ample room' to keep clear. It is important, however, to realise that BL's obligation is not a continuing one. That is to say, when BL establishes her leeward overlap, AW must immediately attempt to keep clear and, if she delays, she will be liable to disqualification under rule 37.1. The following cases refer:

*Holmes* v *Hennig* (RYA 1963/10; IYRU Case 11)

*Tempest* v *Fury Too* (RYA 1963/11)
*Wahoo* v *Susie*; *Susie* v *Wahoo* (RYA 1963/14)
*Caurus* v *Blue Haze*; *Blue Haze* v *Caurus* (RYA 1966/6)
USYRU Appeal No 126, May 13, 1969
Grafham Water Sailing Club (RYA 1970/2)
*Maia* v *Argo* (RYA 1977/5)

With regard to any limitation on BL's freedom of manoeuvre, she is bound by rule 38.2 (Proper Course Limitations), which reads:

> A *leeward yacht* shall not sail above her *proper course* while an *overlap* exists, if when the *overlap* began or, at any time during its existence, the helmsman of the *windward yacht* (when sighting abeam from his normal station and sailing no higher than the *leeward yacht*) has been abreast or forward of the mainmast of the *leeward yacht*.

Obviously, when BL establishes a leeward overlap on AW from clear astern, the helmsman of AW must be forward of BL's mainmast, so that rule 38.2 applies.

Up to and including the 1969 IYRU rules, rule 37.3 ended by saying:

> . . . and during the existence of that *overlap* the *leeward yacht* shall not sail above her proper course.

It will be seen that as, in effect, this says the same thing as the opening words of rule 38.2, which deals with luffing, the IYRU deleted the expression from rule 37.3. The following protest led to the deletion.

One yacht established an overlap to leeward on another from clear astern. Either at the time the overlap was established or at some time during its existence, L was more than two boat lengths to leeward of W. L continued to sail faster than W and, when L was forward of the Mast Abeam position and still more than two boat lengths to leeward of W, L altered course to windward and continued to sail above a proper course, eventually luffing W and causing W to alter course.

At the protest hearing under the rules then in force, W argued quite correctly that, under rule 37.3, L was not permitted to sail above a proper course during the existence of that overlap, which began at the time L established

it on W from clear astern. L argued, also quite correctly, that under rule 38.2 (now 38.3) the overlap began at the time the two yachts closed to within two boat lengths of each other, at which time L was forward of the Mast Abeam position. Under rules 38.1 and 38.2 L was therefore permitted to sail above a proper course and luff W. Both yachts were correct, so the conflict had to be resolved, hence the deletion of the words from rule 37.3.

Nevertheless, when BL establishes an overlap to leeward on AW from clear astern within two boat lengths, the limitation still applies to BL despite the deletion. She must not sail above her proper course, or luff, until she has broken the overlap, either by passing through AW's lee and becoming clear ahead, or by widening out abreast of AW, clearly beyond the two overall lengths mentioned in rule 38.3 (Overlap Limitations), or by losing way and dropping back clear astern of AW.

What all this boils down to is that, although AW, as the windward yacht, is bound by rule 37.1 to keep clear of BL, AW should not be forced to sail above the course which BL was steering at the time she established her overlap.

It must be emphasised that rule 37.3 applies only when BL establishes her overlap to leeward on AW from clear astern. It does not apply, for example, when P and S are meeting close-hauled on opposite tacks and P either crosses ahead of S and tacks to windward of her (weather-bows her), or tacks to leeward of her (lee-bows her), so that when P completes her tack to starboard the two yachts are overlapped on the same tack. Rule 37.3 does not apply in either case, because the overlap was not established from clear astern.

### Examples

In a handicap race (Fig. 19) the 15½ft Kestrel, L, is overtaking the 14ft Bosun, W; both yachts are broad reaching on port tack, some six lengths from the port-hand leeward mark.

In Fig. 20 one Bosun, L, with her spinnaker set, is overtaking another, W, which has no spinnaker. L has established an overlap on W, both yachts running on starboard gybe some

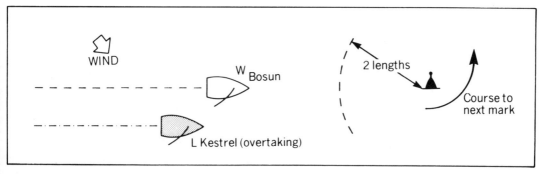

**Fig. 19**

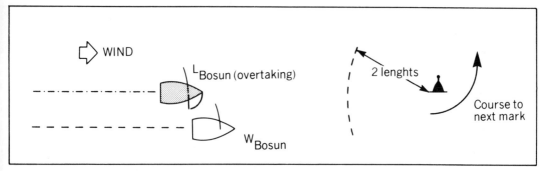

**Fig. 20**

six lengths from a port-hand leeward mark round which they will have to gybe.

Before dealing with each situation separately, some general points can be made. First, the rules governing both situations are the same for yachts of different classes in the same race (in some All Comers handicap races cruisers, half-deckers and dinghies compete against one another) as they are for those of the same class sailing in the same race.

Secondly, the rules are the same for yachts sailing in separate races. When two yachts in different classes racing at the same time come to close quarters and one yacht is much larger than the other, long tradition, courtesy and the unwritten law dictate that the large yacht should pass to leeward of the small one. The helmsman of the large yacht, as a sportsman, should avoid blanketing the small one, causing her as little trouble as possible. Nevertheless, concerning this etiquette, the original point of the law must be observed.

Thirdly, since 1961 the terms 'overtaking' and 'overtaken' have not been used in the rules. The Definitions in the rules refer only to yachts being 'clear astern' and 'clear ahead' of, or 'overlapping' one another.

Turning now to the situation shown in Fig. 19, the rights and obligations of L will be discussed first. She was originally clear astern of W and was bound by the Same Tack—Basic Rule 37.2, When Not Overlapped, which states:

> A yacht *clear astern* shall keep clear of a yacht *clear ahead.*

Next, as soon as L established an overlap to leeward from clear astern on W, rule 37.2 ceased to apply and L became subject to rule 37.3, Transitional, which reads:

> A yacht which establishes an *overlap* to *leeward* from *clear astern* shall allow the *windward yacht* ample room and opportunity to keep clear.

It is well established that the phrase 'ample room and opportunity' means that, in order to fulfil her newly-acquired obligation to keep clear under rule 37.1—When Overlapped (which says: 'A *windward yacht* shall keep clear of a *leeward yacht*'), W is entitled to luff head to wind if she pleases and if, in so doing, any part of her hull, crew or equipment touches any part of L's hull, crew or equipment, that is clear evidence that L has not given W ample room and opportunity to keep clear. The case of Grafham Water Sailing Club (RYA 1970/2) IYRU Case 46, refers.

It is a general principle in the rules that, when the right of way suddenly shifts from one yacht to another, the yacht that has newly acquired the right of way must give the other yacht a fair chance to get clear. Nevertheless, it is also well established that L's obligation under rule 37.3 is not a continuing one; see *Holmes* v *Hennig* (RYA 1963/10; IYRU Case 11).

In the case of *Tempest* v *Fury Too* (RYA 1963/11), illustrated in Fig. 21, the following facts were found. There was no current, and the wind was light and variable. W rounded the mark close to port, just ahead of L, and sailed on a broad reach to clear an obstruction on the course to the next mark. L, after rounding the mark, bore away under W's stern and established an overlap to leeward on W, which was thereafter maintained up to the time of the incident. L luffed to a course

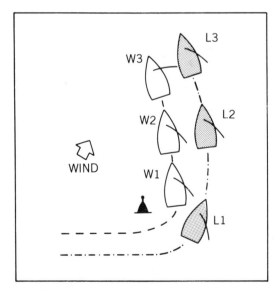

**Fig. 21**

parallel to that of W, and subsequently neither yacht knowingly altered course. After sailing about a length, W pushed her boom out some 12–15 ins, and the block at its end touched L's port shroud. Neither yacht hailed and both protested.

The race committee disqualified L because she was too close to W to allow W to ease her mainsheet; L appealed.

The RYA upheld L's appeal, reversed the race committee's decision and referred to the case of *Holmes* v *Hennig*, pointing out that L's obligation to give W ample room and opportunity to keep clear was not a continuing one and, according to the facts, after L established her leeward overlap on W, W was able to sail about one boat length on a parallel course to L without being forced to alter course to keep clear, and the contact resulted from W pushing her boom out. In the prevailing conditions, these facts supported L's claim to have observed rule 37.3, and suggest that W failed to fulfil her obligation as the windward yacht to keep clear of L. As it was found that L at no time after establishing her leeward overlap on W sailed above her proper course, she complied with rule 38.2 (Proper Course Limitations) which reads:

> A *leeward yacht* shall not sail above her *proper course* while an *overlap* exists, if when the *overlap* began or, at any time during its existence, the helmsman of the *windward yacht* (when sighting abeam from his normal station and sailing no higher than the *leeward yacht*) has been abreast or forward of the mainmast of the *leeward yacht*.

Reverting to the situation shown in Fig. 19, there are several points in rule 38.2 which should be mentioned. First, the proper course for each yacht would be the course made good in the prevailing conditions of wind and tide to reach and round the mark in a seamanlike manner to finish as quickly as possible. Secondly, the existing overlap between L and W continues to exist until it is broken in one of three ways:

(a) By L passing through W's lee and becoming clear ahead.

(b) By L dropping back until she is · clear astern of W.

**Plate 9**   A leeward yacht shall not sail above her proper course if the helmsman of the windward yacht (when sighting abeam from his normal station and sailing no higher than the leeward yacht) has been abreast or forward of the mainmast of the leeward yacht (rule 38.2). But what is normal station?   *Guy Gurney*

(c) By L widening out abreast of W outside two overall lengths in accordance with rule 38.3, Overlap Limitations, which states in part:

> For the purpose of rule 38 only: An *overlap* does not exist unless the yachts are clearly within two overall lengths of the longer yacht.

Let us now look at W's rights and obligations. We already know that, as the windward yacht, she must keep clear of L and that, when L overlaps her to leeward, W can luff to keep clear and if, in doing so she touches L, L has not given her ample room and opportunity to keep clear. In addition, just as L is prohibited by rule 38.2 from sailing above her proper course, so W is prohibited from sailing below her proper course by rule 39 (Same Tack—

Sailing below a Proper Course after Starting), which says:

> A yacht which is on a free leg of the course shall not sail below her *proper course* when she is clearly within three of her overall lengths of either a *leeward yacht* or a yacht *clear astern* which is steering a course to pass to *leeward*.

Note that rule 39 applies only to a free leg of the course. It has been a principle of the rules since 1876 that one yacht may not, by sailing below her proper course, hinder another which is passing her to leeward. Until recently the relevant rules made no distinction between a free leg and a windward leg, and occasional difficulties arose when yachts were close together and beating, one yacht accusing the other of bearing away. Since it frequently proved impossible to decide whether the accused yacht was deliberately sailing below her proper course or was merely being sailed full and fast, rule 39 was re-worded in its present form in 1969.

### Approaching a Mark

Hence the combined effect of rules 38.2 and 39 on the two overlapping yachts in Fig. 19 is to require them to sail approximately parallel courses for the mark. With regard to the situation shown in Fig. 20, the facts that the two yachts are of the same class and that L is carrying her spinnaker and W is not, do not in any way affect their respective rights and obligations that have already been described. The only difference in the rights and obligations of the two situations arise when the two yachts come within two lengths of the mark. In Fig. 19, L has established an outside leeward overlap on W well before they come within two lengths of it. Assuming that the overlap is maintained when they do so, the outside yacht, L, is bound by rule 42.1(a) (Room at Marks and Obstructions when Overlapped), which states:

> An outside yacht shall give each yacht *overlapping* her on the inside, room to round or pass the *mark* or *obstruction*. . . .Room includes room for an *overlapping* yacht to *tack* or *gybe* when either is an integral part of the rounding or passing manoeuvre.

In Fig. 20, the positions are reversed. L is the inside yacht, and W is the outside yacht and must observe rule 42.1(a).

## Establishing a Windward Overlap

In the previous section we discussed rule 37.3, so far as it concerned the situation where a yacht clear astern establishes an overlap to *leeward* on the yacht clear ahead. Let us now study the application of the rules to the other situation where the yacht clear astern goes to *windward*.

### Luffing

As was explained, B (the yacht behind, or clear astern, in Fig. 22), must keep clear of A, the

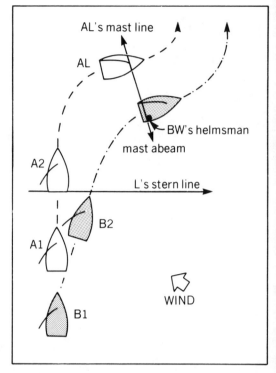

**Fig. 22**

yacht clear ahead, in accordance with rule 37.2. However, rule 38.1 (Luffing Rights) can also apply in this situation. When A either sees that B is about to try to pass her to windward, or waits until BW establishes an overlap to windward on AL, A or AL can luff 'as she pleases' to prevent B or BW from passing her. This is because in either case, in accordance with rule 38.2 (Proper Course Limitations), the helmsman of B or BW is abaft the mastline of A or AL before or when the overlap is established.

The phrase 'as she pleases' means exactly what it says. A or AL can luff without any warning as suddenly and sharply as she pleases, up to head to wind if she chooses—she must not luff beyond head to wind because, according to the definition of tacking, she would begin to tack—and when BW overlaps her, she is allowed to touch BW if she can, provided that no serious damage results, as stated in rule 32 (Avoiding Collisions). AL retains this right until, as shown at the third position in the figure, in accordance with rule

38.2, BW's helmsman (when sighting abeam from his normal station and sailing no higher than the leeward yacht) has been abreast or forward of the mainmast of the leeward yacht. The subject of a helmsman's normal station is discussed under that heading on page 37.

At that moment BW can, in accordance with rule 38.4 (Hailing to Stop or Prevent a Luff), terminate AL's luffing rights by hailing 'Mast Abeam!' or words to that effect, after which AL must immediately bear away to her proper course by heading honestly and fairly for the next mark.

There is an important point of law here. When BW terminates AL's luffing rights and AL bears away, it was ruled in USYRU Appeal No 20 (1 Feb 1946) that:

> A leeward yacht which has luffed a windward yacht as permitted by rule 38.1, may bear away suddenly.

In responding to AL's luff, BW was obligated (under rule 37.1. Author) to keep far enough away from AL so as to give her room to bear away both 'suddenly' and 'rapidly'.

See BW5AL5 in Fig. 23. The RYA cited this interpretation with approval in the case of *Athene* v *Magician* (RYA 1962/29; IYRU Case 3).

In electing to go to windward instead of to leeward, with the deliberate intention of trying to blanket and pass AL, BW should have expected AL to luff her, and she should have been ready to respond. If BW gets 'snicked' in the process, it is her own fault entirely. It is useless for her to complain that AL luffed so suddenly and sharply that she could not keep clear. In coming so close that she could not respond in time, no competent protest committee should have the slightest sympathy with her.

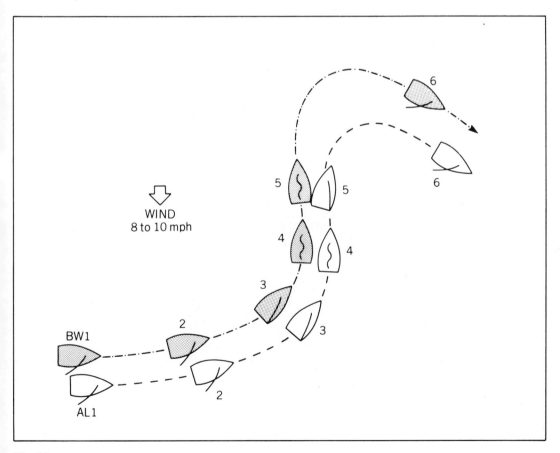

**Fig. 23**

The late Sir William Burton, President of the IYRU and RYA 1937–42, and a famous racing helmsman, laid down the very sound precept that when a yacht clear astern is trying to pass another yacht on the latter's windward side, she should alter course and continue to alter course, so as to keep one-and-a-quarter boat lengths of water between herself and the leeward yacht.

Note that rule 38 is headed 'Same Tack–Luffing and Sailing above a Proper Course after Starting' and that, according to the definition of proper course, there is no proper course before the starting signal. It is also important to understand that rule 38 applies only in open water; AL must not luff BW ashore or into any kind of danger.

With regard to luffing generally, slow luffing is a waste of time and, while it may add zest to the sport, it may be said that more races are lost than are won by sudden luffing. It seldom pays to allow a yacht to come up to windward nearly abeam or more than abreast, and then to luff suddenly with the object of touching her and putting her out of the race, unless an alternative penalty applies. Rule 38, however, permits it. It should be reasonable to suppose that a yacht enters a race for the pleasure, excitement and the battle of wits involved in competing against and trying to beat her opponents. Therefore, luffing should not be used to 'out' an opponent, but solely to prevent her passing. Hence, when A sees that while B is still clear astern she seems to be contemplating

**Plate 10**    If Laser 33496 holds luffing rights on both the yachts immediately astern of her and decides to exercise them, Laser 27198 must respond even if she is Mast Abeam of the intervening International 14 footer with the spinnaker (rule 38.6).                                                      *Tyrer Photography*

coming to windward, A should luff plainly before B gets an overlap at all. That is the seamanlike and sporting way to luff and often causes B to change her mind and go to leeward, because it is a clear indication that if she persists in coming close to windward, she is likely to be luffed head to wind.

Finally, bear in mind the fact that the right-of-way rules are specifically framed to enable yachts to manoeuvre at close quarters in safety. It could be argued that, as the luffing rule seems to invite AL to collide with BW, it hardly conforms with that principle; it certainly is a peculiar rule, but it is a very well known one in racing. The point is that it is seldom a dangerous manoeuvre because, when luffing is allowed, the yachts are sailing approximately parallel courses at much the same speed, and any contact between them tends to be slight and a glancing blow. Moreover, as BW should know very well that if she attempts to pass close to AL and fails to respond to her luff, she will almost certainly be disqualified or penalised in some other way, it can reasonably be claimed that the luffing rule encourages her to avoid collision.

## Mast Abeam

In the case of *Bosun 56* v *Bosun 58* (RYA 1973/3), it was ruled that in a luffing situation the onus lies on the windward yacht to satisfy the race committee that she attained the Mast Abeam position.

An unusual incident occured in an International Star class race during the 1979 Weymouth Olympic Week, between K6290 (L) and E6356 (W). L and W were running on the same port tack, and W established an overlap to windward on L from clear astern. L luffed, W responded and claimed that she hailed L the Spanish equivalent of 'Mast Abeam!'. L said that she heard no hail and assumed that she had the right to continue to luff, which resulted in W's mainsail being draped across L's port rigging and spreader. A third yacht, K6123, abreast of the other two yachts at the time of the incident, also gave evidence.

The protest committee found that, owing to the noise of the sails, any hail by W was not heard by L and, if a hail had been given, it was made before W had attained the Mast Abeam relationship. The protest committee therefore dismissed W's protest on the grounds that a hail must be clearly audible, and disqualified W under rule 37.1 (Same Tack—Basic Rules), for failing to keep clear. In this connection, it was ruled in the case of *N2986* v *N2716* (RYA 1980/6) that a hail must be capable of being heard by the hailed yacht.

## Helmsman's Normal Station

Seeing that the yacht racing rules were first codified by the British Yacht Racing Association in 1875 for use in the United Kingdom; that these rules, in a slightly modified form, were adopted by the International Yacht Racing Union in 1907 for use in Europe; and that since 1961, one code of rules has applied all over the world, it might be thought reasonable to assume that during this period all the permutations and combinations in the relationships between racing yachts would by now have been exhausted. Such, however, is not true, and this section deals with a question that has not often arisen. The only surprise is that, as it concerns normal modern centreboard class racing technique, the subject has not cropped up regularly.

In 1962, after the adoption of one universal code of racing rules, the IYRU instituted a scheme whereby any national authority could submit for international approval and publication as an official IYRU Interpretation of the rules, any case it had decided during the previous year and which it deemed suitable.

At its meeting in November 1979, the IYRU Racing Rules Committee approved ten new cases submitted variously by the Federazione Italiana Vela, the Koninklijk Nederlands Watersport Verbond, the RYA and the USYRU, bringing the total number of Interpretations up to 105. The IYRU publishes these Interpretations in booklet form, with indexes under rule numbers and subjects. They provide a valuable guide to the official applications of the rules, and all members of juries and protest committees should obtain copies for their personal use. This is especially important because IYRU Regulation 6, Racing Rules, para 6.3.3 reads:

> IYRU Interpretations of the Yacht Racing Rules are recognised as authoritative interpretations and explanations of the rules.

## IYRU Official Interpretation

The appeal *Argo* v *Lucky Luke* (IYRU Case 101), national one-design 16M2 class, submitted by the Dutch national authority KNWV will be described because it is unique in that, for the first time in over twenty years since its introduction, an interpretation of the phrase 'the normal station' of the helmsman of a windward yacht regarding the Mast Abeam relationship for terminating a leeward yacht's luffing rights was required.

Up to 1958, a leeward yacht was entitled to luff a windward overtaking yacht 'as she pleased' until the leeward yacht's bowsprit end, or stem if she had no bowsprit, was abaft the mainmast of the windward yacht; after which the leeward yacht could maintain the course she was then steering but could luff no further. This was a difficult relationship for either helmsman to determine with any certainty, because he was stationed at his tiller or wheel some distance from the bowsprit end, stem or mainmast of his yacht. Consequently, many heated and inconclusive arguments as to whether or not the leeward yacht had lost her luffing rights often resulted.

In 1959, largely acting on the advice of Crown Prince Olav of Norway—who later became King Olav V—and strongly supported by the Scandinavian Yachting Union and the President of the IYRU (at that time Mr Peter Scott—later Sir Peter), the IYRU took the first step towards the final goal: to evolve the best racing rules with a view to achieving a universal code as soon as possible, by adopting Part II, Right of Way Rules, from the 1959 Official Racing Rules of the North American Yacht Racing Union. These rules, in a modified form, were those originally known as the Vanderbilt Rules.

Among these new rules were two that tried to solve the problem of terminating luffing rights. They are now rule 38.2 (Proper Course Limitations) and rule 38.4 (Hailing to Stop or Prevent a Luff). Rule 38.2 reads:

> A *leeward yacht* shall not sail above her *proper course* while an *overlap* exists, if when the *overlap* began or, at any time during its existence, the helmsman of the *windward yacht* (when sighting abeam from his normal station and sailing no higher than the *leeward yacht*) has been abreast or forward of the mainmast of the *leeward yacht*.

Rule 38.4 then provides the means of terminating a leeward yacht's luffing rights as follows:

> When there is doubt, the *leeward yacht* may assume that she has the right to *luff* unless the helmsman of the *windward yacht* has hailed 'Mast Abeam', or words to that effect. The *leeward yacht* shall be governed by such hail and, when she deems it improper, her only remedy is to protest.

There seems little doubt that this approach has markedly reduced an earlier twilight zone. The critical determining factor now is the normal station of the helmsman of the windward yacht, and it is interesting to reflect that for more than two decades no one queried where his station might be until it arose in this Dutch appeal.

In my book *The 1959 IYRU Yacht Racing Rules* I wrote: 'With regard to the normal station of the helmsman of the windward yacht. . . .in yachts which are steered with a wheel, or a tiller with no extension, his station must of necessity be fairly circumscribed, but in light displacement craft with tiller extensions, it would appear that it may be more elastic. It is common practice for the helmsmen and crews of such craft to move their weight and position fore and aft according to the course they are sailing and, provided that telescopic spring-loaded tiller extensions or wheel steering forward of the mast are not developed to curtail a leeward yacht's luffing rights, it would seem reasonable to regard such movement of weight and position as coming within the limits of nomality.' Now let's look at that actual Dutch appeal case.

*Facts Found by the Protest Committee*

Both yachts were on a port-tack reach about two metres abreast of one another, W to windward and slightly astern of L. Both yachts believed that L was entitled to luff and she luffed suddenly. While L was luffing, W hailed 'Mast Abeam' but L did not hear this hail and continued to luff until slight contact occurred between the two yachts.

Immediately after contact, both yachts resumed their proper courses. At the moment of contact and while they were on the same course, W's helmsman was just abeam of L's mast. However, W's helmsman was stationed a little forward of her own mainsheet groundblock, while L's helmsman was a little abaft her own groundblock. The majority of helmsmen in this class station themselves forward of the groundblock on a windward leg and abaft it on a downwind leg.

*Conclusions of the Protest Committee*

1. When L started to luff, she was entitled to do so in accordance with rules 38.1 and 38.3 (Same Tack—Luffing and Sailing above a Proper Course after Starting).
2. Rule 38.4 does not cover the situation in which a hail is given but is not heard.
3. In the case of (2) and when the luff continues until contact occurs, the race committee must examine the yachts' positions at the moment of impact.
4. The positions of the yachts as established in (3) will determine whether W kept sufficiently clear in accordance with rule 37.1 (Same Tack—Basic Rule), or whether L infringed rule 38.2.
5. Because the leg was neither a windward nor a downwind one, but a reach, it is considered acceptable that the helmsman's normal station, mentioned in rule 38.2, can vary from yacht to yacht, taking into consideration the existing differences in this respect in the 16M2 class.
6. Summarising, it was clear that at the moment of contact the Mast Abeam position had just been established.

*Decision of the Protest Committee*

On the basis of the foregoing conclusions, L is disqualified for an infringement of rule 38.2.

*Appeal*

In accordance with rule 77.1(c) (Right of Appeal), the race committee asks for a decision of the appeals committee, in particular on the following questions.

(a) Is it correct that rule 38.4 does not cover the situation in which it has been established beyond reasonable doubt that a hail was given but was not heard?
(b) Must the protest committee in such circumstances examine and establish the exact positions of the yachts at the moment of contact?
(c) Are the positions of the yachts at the moment of contact—and especially the fact whether or not at that moment a Mast Abeam situation existed—conclusive for deciding which yacht infringed a rule?
(d) Is it an acceptable fact that the normal station of the helmsman of the windward yacht can vary and need not be the same for all yachts in the same class?

*Decision of the Appeals Committee*

Answers:

(a) Correct, however a hail which has not been heard is inadequate. A second hail is necessary.
(b) No. In case of doubt the leeward yacht has the right to luff.
(c) No. In view of the above answers, the windward yacht infringed rule 37.1.
(d) Yes

'On the basis of the above statements, the decision of the protest committee is reversed. L is reinstated and W disqualified for an infringement of rule 37.1.'

As this case is now an IYRU Interpretation, it is important. The decision stresses the point that the windward yacht, W, is disqualified under rule 37.1 for failing to keep clear of the leeward yacht, L. It implies that W, seeing that L was not responding to W's first hail, should have hailed a second time, loudly, kept clear and if she thought fit, protested against L. Helmsmen should always remember that, in the interests of safety, the rules require them to avoid collision. Equally important in this case, the KNWV's appeals committee's answer to the race committee's question (d)—later confirmed by the IYRU—makes it clear that the normal station of a helmsman can vary according to the class concerned and the prevailing conditions.

However, in any case of doubt, the onus may well lie on the helmsman of a windward yacht who has hailed 'Mast Abeam' to satisfy the race committee that in any given conditions he was at his normal station, and that he had not moved forward to that position in an attempt to justify his hail and thereby terminate the leeward yacht's luffing rights.

By a curious coincidence, just before the IYRU meetings of that year, the Penarth Yacht Club submitted the appeal of *Kundry* v *Trash* (RYA 1980/4), which concerned the same question. In the circumstances, the RYA deferred its consideration of the case until it was known whether or not the IYRU had approved the Dutch appeal. As that became an IYRU Interpretation, the RYA had no difficulty in deciding the British appeal.

## When There is Doubt

Among the cases submitted to the IYRU's Racing Rules Committee at its annual meeting in 1979, for approval as official Interpretations, were four from the United States Yacht Racing Union, one of which was Appeal No 220, *Sundance* v *Haven*, which is now published as IYRU Case 99.

Before considering the appeal itself it may be worthwhile pausing briefly to look at the USYRU's history, and the differences between it and the RYA. The North American Yacht Racing Union originated in 1897, but did not become really active until 1925, when it included the Canadian Yachting Association. In 1975 these two national authorities decided to operate independently, and the NAYRU became the USYRU.

Some readers may wonder how it is that in such a large continent as North America, during the last half-century its national authority has decided only two hundred-odd appeals—an average of roughly four a year—when in the UK the RYA's Racing Rules Committee, which acts as an appeals committee, decides about 50 every year. The difference does not result from the fact that American yachtsmen are more law-abiding or less litigious than the British, but because the constitution of the NAYRU and latterly the USYRU has always differed from that of the RYA.

The USYRU consists of some thirty-eight District Yacht Racing Associations, each of which has its own district appeals committee to which decisions of protests from its constituent clubs are referred for decision. Only after a district appeals committee has decided a case can it be referred to the USYRU Appeals Committee for a final ruling, and it is these cases only that are published as USYRU appeals. The majority of appeals against the decisions of race committees are thus filtered out, and only hitherto unresolved points of law or complicated situations reach the USYRU and are published.

Under the RYA's jurisdiction, however, any recognised club can refer its decisions to the national authority for confirmation, and any individual member of a recognised club can appeal against such a protest committee's decision.

There is also a major difference in the procedures for deciding appeals between the USYRU and the RYA. Owing to the great distances involved, the seven members of the USYRU Appeals Committee conduct their business by correspondence, whereas the twelve members of the RYA Racing Rules Committee meet in London, roughly once a month, to sit round a table for two or three hours and discuss and decide four or five cases at each session.

### Hailing to Stop a Luff

Having, so to speak, cleared the decks for action, let us now deal with the subject of this

**Plate 11** The situation becomes complicated when there are several yachts involved. Overlaps on neighbouring yachts must be considered, and also those affecting nearby yachts which in turn may overlap or be overlapped.     *Studio 77*

section. Rule 38.4 (Hailing to Stop or Prevent a Luff) reads:

> When there is doubt, a *leeward yacht* may assume that she has the right to *luff* unless the helmsman of the *windward yacht* has hailed 'Mast Abeam', or words to that effect. The *leeward yacht* shall be governed by such hail, and, when she deems it improper, her only remedy is to protest.

The Cambridge Cruising Club (RYA 1956/14) asked the following question: 'Should the phrase "when there is doubt" be taken to mean that the windward yacht must respond to a luff whether or not she felt that the leeward yacht was justified in luffing, or on the literal interpretation of the words, only when there is doubt?

The RYA answered: 'A windward yacht fails to respond at her own peril. Under rule 38.4 a windward yacht may avoid this risk by responding, while reserving the right to protest.'

In the case of *Sundance* v *Haven* referred to above (Fig. 24), in light airs *Sundance*, W, established an overlap to windward on *Haven*, L, from clear astern, both yachts running on port tack and W sailing almost twice as fast as L. L luffed and W responded. When W achieved mast abeam on L, W stopped responding and settled on a steady course (above her proper course), but L continued to luff. As

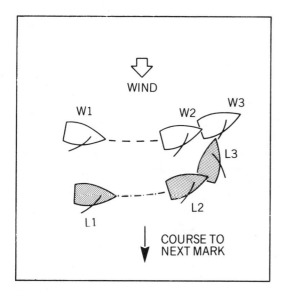

**Fig. 24**

a result there was contact between the two yachts, L's pulpit striking W (or a couple of W's crew fending off) towards the forward end of W's cockpit. A disputed and unresolved fact was whether W's hail of 'Mast Abeam!' came before or after contact.

The USYRU Appeals Committee decided:

> 'Under rule 38.2, the termination of the lee-ward yacht's right to luff occurs when the relative positions of the yachts reach the point where the windward yacht has achieved Mast Abeam.
>
> 'Rule 38.4 operates only when there is doubt as to whether that point has been reached. Where the facts permit no reasonable doubt and establish that the windward yacht actually has achieved Mast Abeam, rule 38.4 does not become operative and the absence of a hail by the windward yacht is of no consequence.
>
> 'That is the situation here. Based upon the point of contact (L's pulpit striking W near the forward end of her cockpit which in W is close to her helmsman's normal station), it is clear that W had reached a position well ahead of Mast Abeam prior to the time of contact, indeed by a sufficient distance that it should have been obvious to L. There thus being no doubt that L's luffing rights had terminated under rule 38.2, she infringed that rule by failing to bear away to her proper course.
>
> 'The decisions of the Protest Committee and the District Appeals Committee are reversed; L is disqualified and W is reinstated.'

The case of *Flight* v *Waves* (RYA 1963/12) is shown in Fig. 25 and is very similar to, and supports, the previous case, except that both yachts were close-hauled. W was passing L to windward on the approach to the first mark. L was sailing closer to the wind than W and therefore travelling more slowly. W responded to L's luff but, when W was forward of the Mast Abeam position, L luffed again and the leech of W's mainsail touched L's forestay. W did not hail 'Mast Abeam' because she did not consider herself close enough to warrant it. L was disqualified for sailing above her proper course when W's helmsman was forward of L's mast.

L appealed on the grounds that rule 37.1 applied and was not sufficiently considered; and that she was disqualified under rule 38.1 with no claim by W that she hailed under rule 38.4. The appeal was dismissed on the grounds

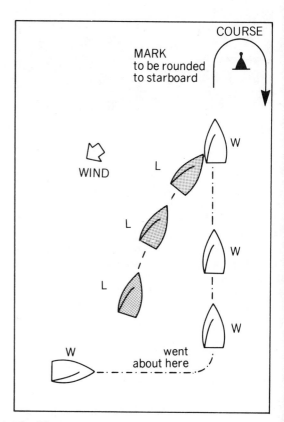

**Fig. 25**

that L could have been in no doubt that, at the time of the incident, she had lost the right to luff.

## Questions

**Q4.1**   When P becomes SL, may she luff SW?

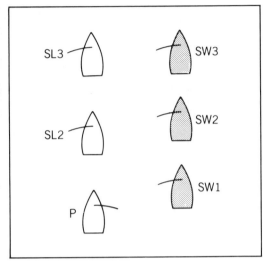

**Fig. Q4.1**

**Q4.2**   If S in Q3.1 (page 24) were an anchored markboat surrounded by navigable water, which both PW and PL must leave to starboard, and PL cannot lay the mark, may she claim room at the mark as overlapping inside yacht, and hail PW about?

**Q4.3**   May L luff at L3?

**Q4.4**   In the situation shown in question 4.3 above, who is wrong if, at W2L2, when L has just established an overlap on W, W decides to put her helm hard down to keep clear and, in the process of turning to starboard, W's boom makes contact with L's shrouds?

**Q4.5**   In the situation shown in question 4.4, is L2's obligation to allow W2 room to keep clear a continuing one?

**Q4.6**   When a yacht clear astern runs up on a yacht clear ahead, and establishes a leeward overlap, what are the rights and obligations of each yacht?

**Q4.7**   What is a 'proper course'?

**Q4.8**   When a small yacht and a large yacht, in separate races, come to close quarters while both are racing, what general principles should apply?

**Q4.9**   Can a leeward yacht with luffing rights luff and touch the windward yacht on which she has rights?

**Q4.10**   When a leeward yacht's luffing rights have been terminated, is she entitled to assume her proper course by bearing away as suddenly and rapidly as she can, and thereby perhaps swinging her stern into the windward yacht and hitting her?

**Q4.11**   Is a helmsman's normal station a fixed one?

**Q4.12**   When there is doubt as to whether a leeward yacht can continue to luff, may she do so?

**Q4.13**   Should the phrase 'When there is doubt' in rule 38.4 be taken to mean that the windward yacht must respond to a luff whether or not she judges that the leeward yacht is justified in so doing, or should it be taken in the literal interpretation of the phrase, only when there is doubt?

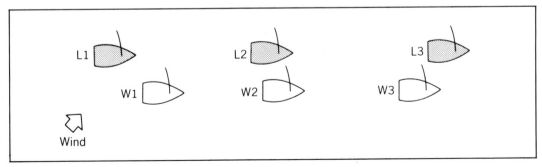

**Fig. Q4.3**

# 5 Tacking and Gybing

As its title implies, rule 41 (Changing Tacks—Tacking and Gybing) is framed to cover the third basic positional relationship, in which one yacht (and sometimes two) is changing tacks either by tacking or by gybing and, in so doing, converts either an opposite-tack situation into a same-tack one or *vice versa*, and so alters the right-of-way relationship between herself and another yacht. The primary object of the rule is to prevent one yacht from tacking or gybing dangerously close to another. It also determines when, after completing a tack or gybe which changes the relationship, a yacht becomes entitled to any rights or is subject to any obligations on her new course, and thus to make conditions as equitable as possible for both yachts.

## Definitions

By definition:

*On a Tack*—A yacht is *on a tack* except when she is *tacking* or *gybing*. A yacht is on the *tack* (*starboard* or *port*) corresponding to her *windward* side.

This means that a yacht is on a tack not only when she is close-hauled, but also when she is reaching or running. In Fig. 26 all the yachts S1–S5 are on starboard tack. The reason that S1 so ranks is explained in the next definition, which reads:

*Tacking*—A yacht is *tacking* from the moment she is beyond head to wind until she has *borne away*, when beating to windward, to a *close-hauled* course; when not beating to windward, to the course on which her mainsail has filled.

Figure 27 shows a close-hauled port-tack yacht, P1, in the process of tacking to starboard. Again by definition:

*Luffing*—Altering course towards the wind.

Hence, from position 1 to position 3, P is luffing; at position 4, as she passed through the eye of the wind or beyond head to wind, she is tacking; when beating to windward she completes her tack when she has borne away to her new close-hauled course; and at position 5 she becomes S, a starboard-tack yacht.

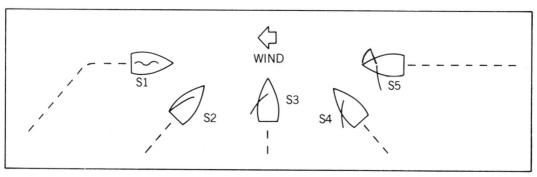

**Fig. 26**

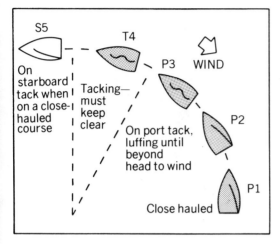

**Fig. 27**

In this connection, an important point was established in the case of the Cyprus Services Sailing Association (RYA 1967/8), namely:

When beating to windward, a yacht has completed her tack when she is heading on a close-hauled course, regardless of her movement through the water or the sheeting of her sails.

There are two reasons for this interpretation. If the definition of tacking required a yacht's sails to be full after tacking before she became entitled to rights on her new close-hauled course, it could be argued that, when her crew caught a riding turn on the winch, so that the headsail could not be fully sheeted in; or when her genoa back-winded the luff of the mainsail so that it was not full, she had not completed her tack, and therefore was not entitled to any rights on her new course.

Figure 28 shows a port-tack yacht, P1, in the process of gybing to starboard. Two definitions are relevant:

*Bearing Away*—Altering course away from the wind until a yacht begins to *gybe*

and also:

*Gybing*—A yacht begins to *gybe* at the moment when, with the wind aft, the foot of her mainsail crosses the centre line, and completes the *gybe* when the mainsail has filled on the other *tack*.

The foot of her mainsail is used instead of the boom, to cover a loose-footed mainsail. P1 therefore continues to be on port tack from position 1 to position 3; is gybing as soon as the foot of her mainsail crosses her centre line, as shown at G1 and G2; has completed her gybe when her mainsail has filled and is on starboard tack at S.

Subject to rule 41 (detailed below) S5 in Fig. 27 can claim to have completed her tack when she is on her new close-hauled course, and S in Fig. 28 can claim to have completed her gybe when her mainsail has filled on the other tack. As will be explained, however, it does not necessarily follow in either case that at that moment she becomes entitled to starboard-tack rights.

## Tacking

Let us now study Fig. 29, which shows the first of several opposite-tack situations that can

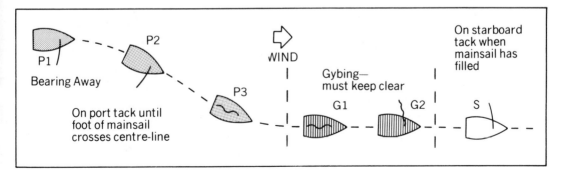

**Fig. 28**

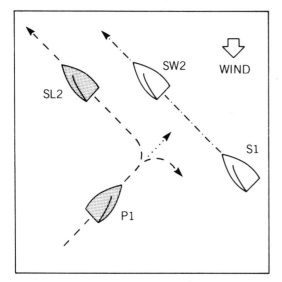

**Fig. 29**

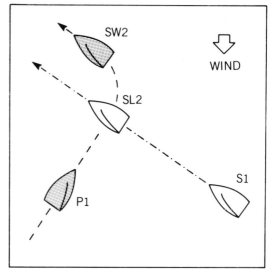

**Fig. 30**

often occur on a beat, when the close-hauled port-tack yacht, P1, meets the close-hauled starboard-tack yacht, S1, and P1 is bound by rule 36 (Opposite Tacks—Basic Rule) to keep clear. P1 can keep clear in one of several ways. First, by bearing away and passing under S1's stern—and in many cases this is the safe and seamanlike course to adopt. However, if P1 does bear away, she may from the tactical point of view sacrifice much valuable and hard-won weather gage. Secondly, P1 can ease sheets and lose just enough way to let S1 cross clear ahead of her. Thirdly, P1 may have the choice of tacking in one of three ways.

1. If she is sufficiently in the lead, she can cross clear ahead of S and then, if she wishes, tack to starboard on S1's weather bow as shown in Fig. 30 at SW2SL2.
2. She can tack dead ahead of S, 'in her water' as shown in Fig. 31 at SA2SB2.
3. When P1 cannot risk either of these manoeuvres, she can tack to leeward of S, on S1's lee bow as shown in Fig. 29 at SL2SW2.

## When is a Tack Completed?

Provided that P does not weather-bow nor lee-bow S too closely, neither the first nor the

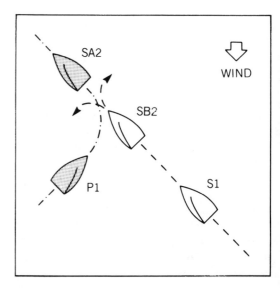

**Fig. 31**

third manoeuvre is potentially dangerous because, when P has completed her tack, she will be sailing a course parallel to S. Both these manoeuvres are effective methods of attack, but the most lethal method of all is for P to tack dead ahead of S, as shown in Fig. 31 at SA2SB2. However, unless SA2 can complete her tack to starboard far enough ahead of SB2, so that SB2 is not suddenly forced to alter course by luffing or bearing away to avoid a collision, it is a dangerous and unseamanlike manoeuvre and one which rule 41 is designed to prohibit.

Figure 29 shows how, after P1 has completed her tack and lee-bows S1 at SL2SW2, the right of way originally held by S1 under rule 36 (Opposite Tacks—Basic Rule) is transferred to SL2 under rule 37.1 (Same Tack—Basic Rules, When Overlapped), and SW2 must now keep clear. In addition, as the helmsman of SW2 is abaft the mainmast of SL2, the latter has luffing rights under rule 38.1 (Same Tack—Luffing and Sailing above a Proper Course after Starting).

Figure 30 shows how, after P1 has completed her tack and weather-bows S1 at SL2SW2, although the right of way originally held by S1 ceases, S1 (now SL2) becomes the leeward yacht and the right of way is retained by her, but now under rule 37.1, so that P1 (now SW2) must still keep clear.

Figure 31 shows how, after P1 has completed her tack dead ahead of S1 at SA2SB2, the right of way originally held by S1 under rule 36 ceases. P1 (now SA2) becomes the yacht clear ahead, and the right of way is transferred to her under rule 37.2 so that S1 (now SB2) must keep clear.

How best to fulfil the requirements of both safety and equity in the situation shown in Fig. 31 has exercised the minds of the rule-makers over a long period, and has resulted in various rule changes. Perhaps a description of those changes and the reasons for them may be of interest, and may help yachtsmen to understand the problems involved.

The first rule governing this situation and others of a similar kind appeared in the IYRU's original code in 1908, as a provision in rule 30 (Right of Way) which read:

> (i) A yacht may not tack so as to involve risk of collision with another yacht before filling on her new tack; nor so as to involve risk of collision with another yacht which, owing to her position, cannot keep clear.

In 1912 the Yacht Racing Association added a footnote to this rule, for UK use, which read:

> A yacht which tacks so close to another as not

to be able to gather full way before a collision would occur, must be disqualified.

There were a number of these footnotes to rule 30, which simply explained how the YRA would interpret and apply the rules as they then stood; they were not intended to bind other national authorities in any way. It will be noted that the 1908 rule used the phrase 'before filling on her new tack', whereas the YRA footnote read 'gather full way before. . .', a significant modification which seemed to fulfil the safety requirement alone. This rule and its YRA footnote remained in force until, in 1930, they were amended and combined to read as follows:

> *Altering Course* (I) A yacht may not tack so as to involve probability of collision with another yacht unless she can gather full way on her new tack before a collision would occur; nor so as to involve probability of collision with another yacht which, owing to her position, cannot keep out of the way. A yacht which tacks so close in front of another as to cause the latter to alter course to avoid a collision before the former has gathered full way must be disqualified.

At this time, the New York Yacht Club and the NAYRU first agreed to adopt right-of-way rules that followed the 1930 IYRU rules, and they were discussing with the YRA the question: 'When does a yacht that has tacked become entitled to her rights on her new tack?' The relevant American rule at the time read:

> A yacht shall not become entitled to her rights on a new course until she has filled away.

Although 'full way' and 'filled away' were different expressions, both sides agreed that in a general sense they were intended to caution the tacking yacht against tacking when there is not room. They also agreed that, owing to the varying sizes and types of vessels and the differing condition of wind and sea, it was impossible to frame a rule which stated that a vessel could either safely tack, or gather full way, or have filled away at any prescribed distance from another vessel.

On the one hand, the Americans disliked the expression 'full way' because they said that in

America it would be taken to mean full speed, that is, the tacking yacht must gather the same speed on her new tack as she had on her original tack before tacking. This went beyond the British interpretation of full way, particularly when it was alleged that Harold S Vanderbilt—three times the successful defender of the America's Cup—said that sometimes a J class yacht did not regain full speed on her new tack for about a quarter-of-an-hour after tacking.

On the other hand, although the British did not want the tacking yacht to be required to regain full speed in order to be able to claim her rights, they disliked the expression 'filled away' for two reasons. First, because it might be taken in Great Britain to mean tacked and only just filled her sails on the new tack—a meaning which the majority of the Americans themselves did not intend. Secondly, it was felt that the expression itself was not in common use amongst British yachtsmen—apparently overlooking the fact that, from 1908 to 1929, IYRU rule 30(i) used the expression 'before filling on her new tack.'

There being reasonable objections to both expressions, the conference accepted a new expression, 'proper way', a compromise between the two discarded ones. Although the new expression was less precise than either of the previous ones, it was less restrictive than full way, and its very lack of precision discouraged one yacht from tacking too close to another. Consequently, in 1934, the term 'proper way' replaced the term 'full way' in rule 30(I), which otherwise remained unchanged until, in 1959, rule 33.3 (Tacking and Gybing)—now rule 41—was adopted. It reads:

## 41    Changing Tacks—Tacking and Gybing

41.1    BASIC RULE
A yacht which is either *tacking* or *gybing* shall keep clear of a yacht *on a tack*.

41.2    TRANSITIONAL
A yacht shall neither *tack* nor *gybe* into a position which will give her right of way unless she does so far enough from a yacht *on a tack* to enable this yacht to keep clear without having to begin to alter her course until after the *tack* or *gybe* has been completed.

41.3    ONUS
A yacht which *tacks* or *gybes* has the onus of satisfying the race committee that she completed her *tack* or *gybe* in accordance with rule 41.2.

41.4    WHEN SIMULTANEOUS
When two yachts are both *tacking* or *gybing* at the same time, the one on the other's port side shall keep clear.

Note that when rule 41.2 is applied to a yacht which tacks on a beat, none of the three earlier terms is used. A new concept is introduced which favours equity at the expense of safety—a change in principle that resulted from the adoption of the NAYRU right-of-way rules in force in 1959 (a change that was accepted with reluctance by the British members of the IYRU Racing Rules Committee at the time, because it allowed one yacht to tack dead ahead of another much closer than before).

Let us now look at the situation shown in Fig. 32. At position 1, because PB1 (the yacht clear astern) and PA1 (the yacht clear ahead) are sailing parallel courses, there is little risk of collision; PA1 holds right of way under rule 37.2. Should PB1 subsequently establish an overlap to windward, PA1 then holds right of way under rule 37.1 and has luffing rights under rule 38.1. If PA1 now tacks onto starboard tack as shown at P2S2, a new changing-tack and then an opposite-tacks situation begin.

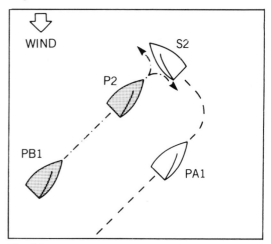

**Fig. 32**

**Plate 12**   Each of these 470's at the '79 WOW series will be defined as gybing from the moment the foot of her mainsail crosses the centre line, until the mainsail has filled on the port tack – the position of the spinnaker has no significance when determining the tack (but rule 54.3 says that the spinnaker boom shall be carried on the side of the mast opposite to the main boom, except when it is being shifted). As such, both dinghies must keep clear of others on a tack (rule 41.1); Britain's K491 would appear not to be clear astern of the New Zealander ahead of her, so the former has right of way as between the two gybing yachts (rule 41.4 says that when two yachts are both gybing at the same time, the one on the other's port side shall keep clear).

*Alastair Black*

In the situations shown in Figs. 31 and 32 the tacking yacht, P1 or PA1, must, while she is tacking, keep clear of SB2 or P2, and she must complete her tack far enough away from the yacht on a tack (SB2 in Fig. 31 and P2 in Fig. 32), so that the latter is not required to begin to alter course until the former has completed her tack. The latter must then have room to keep clear, either by luffing or by bearing away. The important difference between the present rule and 1934 rule 30(I) is that, under the earlier rule, when the yacht on a tack held her course and could touch the yacht ahead of her, the latter would in many cases have been disqualified for not having gathered proper way. Under the present rule, taking into consideration the characteristics of the yachts involved and the prevailing conditions of wind and sea, the tacking yacht complies with rule 41.2 provided that the race committee is satisfied that the yacht on a tack was not forced to begin to alter course to avoid a collision before the tack was completed. If in these circumstances the yacht on a tack held her course and touched the yacht ahead of her, the yacht holding her course would be disqualified under rule 37.2 or under rule 36.

In connection with tacking dead ahead of another yacht, it may be of interest to observe that in 1960, when for the first time the present rule was in force in the Olympics (at Naples), nearly all yachts approached the windward mark close-hauled on the starboard tack; in 1964 (after helmsmen had become familiar with the rule), in the Enoshima Olympics about half the fleet approached the mark on starboard tack and the remainder came in on port tack and tacked dead ahead of the starboard-tack yachts, resulting in a number of protests by the latter—some of which were upheld and some dismissed. In the case of the Takapuna Sailing Club (RYA 1963/15 IYRU Case 12), the RYA commented that 'too narrow an interpretation of this rule is likely to lead to bad seamanship. . .'

## Gybing

Having discussed tacking, we must now deal with gybing, because a yacht can also acquire right of way by so doing. With regard to Fig. 33, the first point to note is that rule 37.2 is a same-tack rule and therefore, although S1 is clear astern of P1, they are in an opposite-tack situation in which P1 must keep clear of S1 under rule 36. However, assuming that P1 can safely cross ahead of S1 and that she keeps clear while gybing onto starboard tack, when P1 has completed her gybe in accordance with rule 41.2, rule 36 ceases to apply and rule 37.2 comes into force, under which S1 (now SB2) as the yacht clear astern must keep clear of P1 (now SA2).

As explained on page 21, because the tacking or gybing yacht initiates a new situation for which she alone is responsible, rule 41.3 places the onus on her of satisfying the race committee that she complied with rule 41.2. Finally, rule 41.4 covers the situation in which two yachts tack or gybe at the same time, and

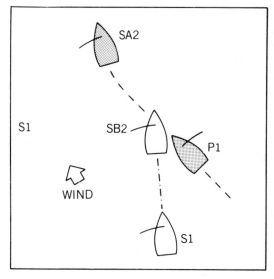

**Fig. 33**

requires the one on the other's port side to keep clear.

## Questions

**Q5.1**   When does a gybe begin?

**Q5.2**   When is a gybe completed?

**Q5.3**   Who has right of way between two yachts gybing?

**Q5.4**   When does a yacht rank as starting to tack?

**Q5.5**   When is a tack completed?

**Plate 13**   When jockeying for position on a run to a leeward mark, there is a possibility that some yachts may gybe onto starboard. If this happens, a right-of-way yacht could find that she has not only lost any luffing rights, but she could be constrained by rule 35 (Limitations on Altering Course).   *David Eberlin*

# 6 Starting

## Proper Course

It is important that helmsmen and race committees should realise that rule 38 (Same Tack—Luffing and Sailing above a Proper Course after Starting) and rule 39 (Same Tack—Sailing below a Proper Course after Starting) do not come into effect until *after* a yacht has started, and that the definition of 'proper course' states:

There is no *proper course* before the starting signal.

Nevertheless, some helmsmen apparently fail to grasp these facts because, before the start, some leeward yachts quite wrongly luff windward yachts suddenly, and vociferously object when windward yachts bear away towards them. Actually, although it may be a risky manoeuvre, there is no rule which prohibits a windward yacht from bearing away *before* the starting signal—always provided that she observes the Same Tack—Basic Rule 37.1, windward yacht keeps clear.

The reasons for these limitations are not difficult to appreciate. Once two yachts on the same tack have started and cleared the starting line, and are on course for the first mark, it is a relatively simple matter to determine how they came into any particular relationship to one another, because they have been sailing in the same direction at roughly the same speed. But during that most exciting and confused period between the preparatory and starting signals, all yachts are striving to get a good start. They often luff, tack, gybe and bear away with such bewildering frequency and speed that it is impracticable to try to apply the principles of

rules 38 and 39; it also explains why it is difficult to say what course any given yacht is sailing, and almost impossible to determine whether or not in the circumstances that course is a proper one. Consequently, for the sake of simplicity, there is a rule governing the manoeuvres of a leeward right-of-way yacht until she has started and cleared the starting line; it reads:

### 40  Same Tack—Luffing before Starting

Before a right-of-way yacht has *started* and cleared the starting line, any *luff* on her part which causes another yacht to have to alter course to avoid a collision shall be carried out slowly and in such a way as to give a *windward yacht* room and opportunity to keep clear. However, the *leeward yacht* shall not so *luff* above a *close-hauled* course, unless the helmsman of the *windward yacht* (sighting abeam from his normal station) is abaft the mainmast of the *leeward yacht*. Rules 38.4 (Hailing to Stop or Prevent a Luff); 38.5 (Curtailing a Luff); and 38.6 (Luffing Two or more Yachts) also apply.

The first point to stress is that any luff during the five-minute period before the starting signal must be carried out slowly. Secondly, when the helmsman of the windward yacht is forward of the Mast Abeam position, the leeward yacht may luff slowly up to close-hauled, provided that she gives the windward yacht 'room and opportunity to keep clear.' Thirdly, when the helmsman of the windward yacht is abaft the Mast Abeam position, the leeward yacht may luff slowly up to head to wind, subject to the same proviso. In either situation, the windward yacht may be forced to start prematurely in order to keep clear—she cannot claim that the starting line is an ob-

**Plate 14** The limitations on a yacht's right to alter course change at the starting signal. After it, she may assume her proper course, and other yachts must assume that she will do this and allow her room to do so. Before she has started and cleared the starting line, she may alter course (e.g. luff) only slowly and, after the starting signal, she may not sail above the compass bearing of the course to the first mark, or above close-hauled, in order to deprive a windward yacht of room at a starting mark surrounded by navigable water. Rules 40 and 42.4 refer.                                                   *David Eberlin*

struction. Finally, because there is a proper course after the starting signal, from that moment a leeward yacht, even abaft the Mast Abeam position, is entitled to assume her proper course, and the windward yacht is bound by rule 37.1 to keep clear.

At L1W1 in Fig. 34, during the starting manoeuvres L has established an overlap to leeward on W. If the yachts are not close-hauled and the course to the first mark is a beat, L can luff slowly to a close-hauled course, even though the helmsman of W is forward of the Mast Abeam position so that L has no luffing rights; W must keep clear under rule 37.1. At L2W2, as W's helmsman is abaft the Mast Abeam position, L can now luff slowly up to head to wind if she pleases. Finally, at L3W3 the overlap continues between L and W. Because L, the leading yacht, has started, rule 38.3 (Overlap Limitations) says that the overlap is regarded as a new one beginning at that time, so that L (who has started and cleared the starting line) may now luff W (whose helmsman is abaft the Mast Abeam position) 'as she pleases' in accordance with rule 38.1.

### Barging

Let us now study what was originally an American rule, often called the anti-barging

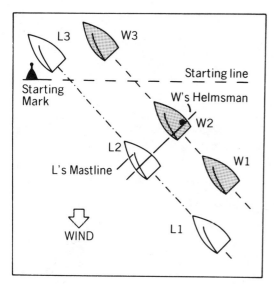

**Fig. 34**

rule, and adopted by the IYRU in 1950. It reads:

42.4    AT A STARTING MARK SURROUNDED BY NAVIG-
ABLE WATER
When approaching the starting line to *start*, a *leeward yacht* shall be under no obligation to give any *windward yacht* room to pass to leeward of a starting *mark* surrounded by navigable water; but, after the starting signal, a *leeward yacht* shall not deprive a *windward yacht* of room at such a *mark* by sailing either above the compass bearing of the course to the first *mark* or above *close-hauled*.

As the common name of this rule implies, its object is to prevent a windward overlapping yacht from barging in at a starting mark on a leeward yacht. Note that when the sailing instructions denote a starting line in accordance with rule 6(c) (Starting and Finishing Lines) as:

the extension of a line through two stationary posts, with a *mark* at or near its outer limit, inside which the yachts shall pass

and these posts or beacons are situated on the shore, as shown in Fig. 35, or on a pierhead, this anti-barging rule cannot be used at the inner end of the starting line, although it will apply at its outer end.

Prior to the adoption of this rule, it used to be—most regrettably sometimes still is—a common practice for yachts to manoeuvre high to windward of the starting mark during the final minute or so before the starting signal. Then, steering free, they would converge on a leeward right-of-way yacht, L, that is steering a course to cross the starting line at its windward end, and most unfairly establish an inside overlap at the starting mark, as shown by W's course in Figs. 35 and 36, thereby snatching from L the coveted windward berth, or pin position, at the start.

In Fig. 35 on a reaching start, and in Fig. 36 on a close-hauled start, the fact that M has established a windward inside overlap on L well before the starting line is reached, is of no significance, because rule 42.1 (Rounding or Passing Marks and Obstructions) reads:

When yachts are about to round or pass a *mark*, other than a starting *mark* surrounded by navigable water, on the same required side. . .

As windward yachts under rule 37.1, both M and W must keep clear of L by either easing sheets, losing way and dropping into L's wake, or passing to windward of the starting mark, taking a round turn and then starting. Any windward yacht in the position of M or W which barges in on L and touches her or the mark, or both, infringes rule 37.1 or else rule 52.1 (Touching a Mark), or she may infringe both.

Figs. 35 and 36 show L to be making a perfectly judged start, crossing the starting line close to the starting mark at full speed a second or so after the starting signal has been made, and the only limitation on her, as has been explained, is that before she starts she can alter course only slowly. Nevertheless, if she has luffing rights as shown in Figs. 35 and 36, before the starting signal she can either sail above the course for the first mark if the wind be free, or luff slowly head to wind, if the first leg of the course is a beat, in attempting to consign M and W to outer darkness while during the same process making a perfect start herself.

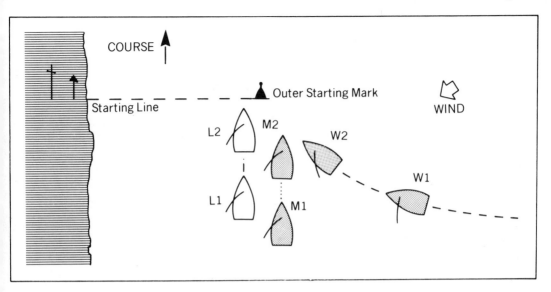

**Fig. 35**

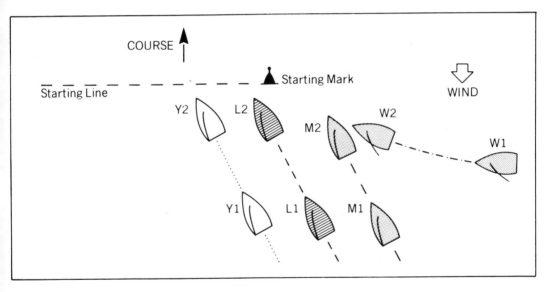

**Fig. 36**

Note that USYRU Appeal No 184 states:

As defined, 'proper course' could be one of several courses at any given moment, depending on the particular circumstances involved. The defined term 'proper course' is found in many rules. However, it is nowhere to be found in rule 42.4. According to this rule, after the starting signal a leeward yacht shall not deprive a windward yacht of room at a starting mark by sailing above *the course* to the first mark. The course to the first mark, as opposed to a proper course, can only mean one thing: the compass course or the rhumb line course to the first mark.

So much for the perfect start. But suppose the starting signal is made when L is still some distance from the starting mark, what then? If she is steering a course for the first mark with a free wind, or is close-hauled to beat up the first leg of the course, she need do nothing and can hold her course to cross the starting line. However, as shown in Fig. 37, L may have planned to pass close to the starting mark as the starting signal was made, and in the wind-

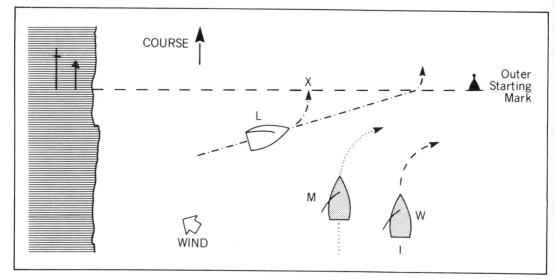

**Fig. 37**

ward berth, then bear away onto her course for the first mark. She is entitled to sail this course up to the starting signal, and M and W must keep clear so, if she reaches the mark just before the starting signal is made, she can carry out her plan. But if she has misjudged speed and distance, immediately the starting signal is made she is bound by rule 42.4 not to deprive M and W of room at the mark by sailing above the course to the first mark. Hence, if the starting signal is made when the yachts are in the positions shown in Fig. 37, L is not necessarily required to bear away immediately to cross the starting line at the nearest point, X, and she can hold her course until she reaches such a position that she would deprive M and W of room at the mark if she continued any further, so at that point she must bear away and give M and W the necessary room.

Similarly, in a close-hauled start as shown in Fig. 36, if the starting signal is made when the yachts are in position 1, L must thereafter sail a *bona fide* close-hauled course to start and, in accordance with rule 42.4, she may not luff above it to deprive M and W of room at the mark. But if, in holding her *bona fide* close-hauled course to position 2, there is no room

for M or W to pass the mark on the same required side, they cannot claim room and must keep clear.

Should there be a fourth yacht (Y in Fig. 36) to leeward of L, Y would be subject to the same limitations with regard to L, as L is with regard to M and W, but with one important difference: as L would have room to pass the mark on the same required side, L could start although neither M nor W could. With regard to this point, USYRU Appeal No 38 states:

Ignorance of the rules is no excuse for the infringement of any rule. . . .it is an established principle of yacht racing that when a yacht voluntarily or unintentionally makes room available to another yacht which has no right under the rules to such room, nor makes or indicates any claim to it, such as to pass between her and a mark. . ., the other yacht may take advantage, at her own risk, of the room so given.

Section 2, Altering Course, dealt with a starboard-tack yacht tacking to assume a proper (close-hauled) course to start as soon as the starting signal is made (Fig. 5) and the need to allow room and opportunity for others to keep clear, so that situation will not be discussed again here.

**Plate 15** If these 470's have to leave the outer distance mark to starboard when they start, they are all fanning and the anti-barging rule (42.4) will come into play. K490 will be under no obligation after the starting signal to give any windward yacht room to pass to leeward of the mark; after the starting signal she must not sail above the compass bearing of the course to the first mark or above close-hauled, and all those to windward of her must expect that she will do this.                              *Basil G Emmerson*

The last situation relating to room at the starting mark is shown in Fig. 38. L and W are approaching the starting line to start, close-hauled and overlapping on the same starboard tack. W can fetch the port-end starting mark, while L cannot. Because the right-of-way yacht, L, has not started, and because W's helmsman is forward of the Mast Abeam position, L is prohibited by rule 40 from sailing above a close-hauled course, that is, luffing, to shoot the mark. She must either ease sheets to drop clear astern of W, and then luff and shoot the mark if she has enough way on to do so, or make a round turn and then start. This holds

good even after the starting signal, until L satisfies the definition of starting:

A yacht *starts* when. . ., after her starting signal, any part of her hull, crew or equipment first crosses the starting line in the direction of the course to the first *mark*.

The situation in Fig. 38 bears a family resemblance to that covered by rule 43.3 (Limitation on Right to Room when the Obstruction is a Mark), which prohibits L from hailing W for room to tack round the mark, when W can fetch it. As L's position is a fairly disastrous one, she should exercise intelligent

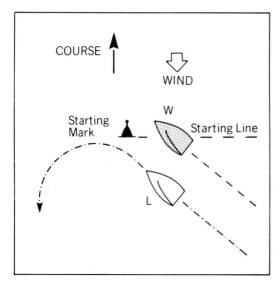

COURSE

WIND

W

Starting Mark

Starting Line

L

**Fig. 38**

anticipation and escape from the situation well before reaching the mark.

However, if W were abaft the Mast Abeam position, so that L had the right to luff up to head to wind and the starting signal had been made, rendering rule 40 inapplicable and bringing rule 38.1 and the definition of proper course into effect, L could claim that, in the absence of W, her proper course would have been to luff and shoot the mark and if W were there, she would be required to keep clear.

## Starting Marks

A race committee that lays a starting limit (distance) mark on the pre-start side of the starting line should know by this time that it will almost certainly cause trouble. The ruling case on this situation occurred over forty-five years ago at the start of an International Six-Metre class race at Burnham-on-Crouch under the burgee of The Royal Corinthian Yacht Club (YRA 1933/9). The sailing instructions defined the starting line as being 'between the Shore Ends buoy and two marks on shore'. This wording was used because it was known that the buoy could not be kept on

the transit of the two beacons on shore for both flood and ebb tides, and the usual wording of 'a line drawn between two marks on shore' was purposely omitted.

In a light wind, after the preparatory signal had been made, two yachts luffed up between the buoy and the transit line for a considerable distance and, when the starting signal was made, they crossed the transit line well to windward of the buoy and the other yachts that started normally; see Fig. 39.

As these two yachts did not start 'between the Shore Ends buoy and the two marks on shore', the race committee decided that they did not start in accordance with the sailing instructions and must be disqualified. The race committee maintained that if in such circumstances yachts were allowed to start and finish anywhere on the line, the whole intention and use of a limit mark would disappear. However, as the race was an important one, the race committee referred its decision under what is now rule 77.1(c) (Appeals) to the Council of the Yacht Racing Association, which tersely ruled that 'the yachts were quite within their rights and should not be disqualified'.

On the face of it, the race committee may seem to have had reasonable grounds for its decision, but the Council would have none of it. The two yachts took the starting line to be the prolongation of the transit of the two shore beacons and they passed the limit mark as prescribed in the sailing instruction, but by luffing up to windward of that mark they gained a great advantage. Obviously it was impossible to draw a straight line between the limit mark and the two shore beacons because these three points were not in line. The situation could not have arisen if either the limit mark had been laid on the course side of the starting line, or the line had been between the limit mark and one beacon on shore. It became known as a 'Corinthian' start, and the case was cited by the Council in the similar case of the Shaldon Sailing Club (YRA 1951/11).

It was not until the appeal of *Psyche* v Race Committee (RYA 1965/18)—illustrated in Fig. 40—was decided by the Council that it gave its reasons for so doing, as follows:

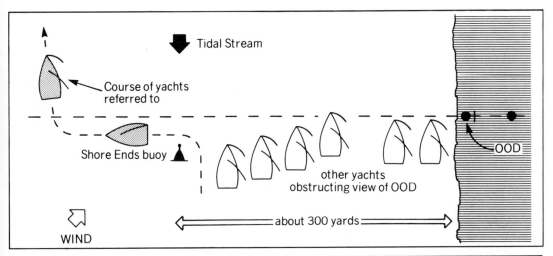

**Fig. 39**

By definition a yacht starts when, *after her starting signal*, any part of her hull, crew or equipment first crosses the starting line in the direction of the first mark.

As neither rule 51.2 nor rule 51.3 (Sailing the Course) applies until a yacht starts she cannot be disqualified if, *before she starts*, she passes a starting mark on what would later be the required side and starts outside that mark.

The cases of the Royal Corinthian Yacht Club (YRA 1933/9) and the Shaldon Sailing Club (YRA 1951/11) refer.

If the race committee cannot lay the Inner Distance Mark, IDM, exactly on the starting line, it should be laid on the 'wrong' side of, or over, the starting line, so that in starting, a yacht must cross the starting line before passing the IDM on the required side.

Alternatively, it might be possible to lay *two* IDMs and *two* ODMs (one on each side of the starting line) and to prescribe that they be passed on the required side when starting, so that whatever the state of the tide, one would be over the starting line.

There are two points to note about this decision. First, the rules no longer refer to the 'right' and 'wrong' sides of, or 'over', the starting line, but more precisely to the 'pre-start' and 'course' sides of it. Secondly, when this appeal was decided, the third sentence of what is now rule 51.3 had not been inserted. It reads:

> A starting limit *mark* has a required side for a yacht from the time she is approaching the starting line to *start* until she has left it astern on the first leg.

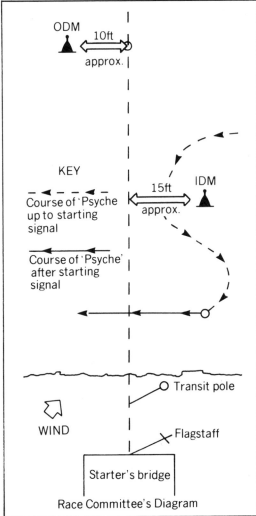

**Fig. 40**

This was added in 1973 to try to help a race committee that had laid a starting mark on the pre-start side of the starting line. In practice, it may not have achieved its objective because it is imprecise. It may serve when a yacht starts by crossing the starting line at right angles, but in a conventional windward start, a close-hauled yacht crosses the line at an angle of about 45°, and at what moment is she 'approaching' the starting line when she reaches parallel to it on the pre-start side?

In 1975, the Royal Ocean Racing Club asked the following questions regarding the legality of certain starting manoeuvres when a starting mark is on the pre-start side of the starting line; they gave as facts: 'The starting line is a transit and the sailing instructions require the starting limit mark, SLM, to be left to starboard (see Fig. 41). No yacht is on the course side of the starting line when the starting signal is made.

'A. on port tack, passes between SLM and the transit line after the preparatory signal is made. She remains on port tack and starts.

'B. on port tack, passes between SLM and the transit line after the preparatory signal is made. She tacks onto starboard and starts.

'C. on port tack, passes between SLM and the transit line after preparatory signal is made. She remains on port tack but crosses the starting line to the course side and returns across it before the starting signal is made.

'D. on port tack, crosses the transit line, leaves SLM to starboard after the preparatory signal is made, returns across the transit line on the outer side of SLM and starts on port tack.

'(NB. It appears that C's and D's courses differ in degree and not in kind, although in D's case the SLM could be on the course side of the starting line.)'

The RORC posed the following questions:

'1. Can any of the four yachts be disqualified under rule 51.3 and, if so, which?

'2. What would be the difference if the SLM were: (a) 10 yards on the pre-start side of the starting line, (b) 100 yards on the pre-start side of the starting line?

'3. How is the phrase: from the time she is

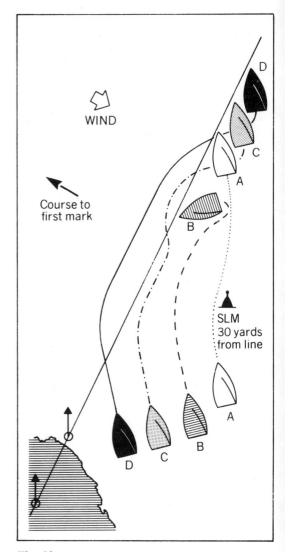

**Fig. 41**

*approaching* the starting line to start until. . .' to be interpreted in each case, with particular reference to the word "approaching"?'

The answer was as follows:

'The principle to be observed is described in YR!/78, International Yacht Racing Rules, Appendix 12, Organisation of Principal Events, Section 7, Championship Race or Races (This appendix is no longer included in either the 1981 IYRU's booklet, or the RYA booklet YR1/81). Under (d) Starting Line, para. (iii), page 96 (also in the 1977 rules booklet, page 81, same heading), namely, that the starting limit marks must always be laid either *on* the transit line or, if that be impracticable, *on the course side of it*, so as to obviate difficulties of the kind described.

'Adherence to this principle ensures that the length of the starting line is effectively limited because yachts when starting must pass the SLM on the required side.

'In accordance with the definition of starting and rule 51.2, a string representing a yacht's wake from the time she starts must lie on the required side of the SLM.

'If the SLM is so far from the starting line that a yacht can pass it before she starts, it then has no required side and does not rank as a mark.

'Answers to questions:

1. No

2. (a) None. (b) None.

3. In the light of the answers to Questions 1 and 2, question 3 is not relevant.'

It must be understood that the answers assume that rule 51.1(c), the 'Round the Ends' rule, was not in force, and the reference to the Organisation of Principal Events has been updated to conform to the latest editions of the RYA and IYRU booklets.

In 1977 the Clyde Yacht Clubs' Association asked whether it was correct that, because the starting limit mark is on the pre-start side of the starting-line, it did not rank as a mark and therefore could be disregarded. The RYA answered that the statement is correct only provided that the mark is more than one overall boat's length on the pre-start side of the starting line.

IYRU racing rules 51.2 and 51.3 (Sailing the Course) jointly require that a string representing the wake of a yacht, from the time she is approaching the starting line to start until she has started and left the limit mark astern, shall lie on the required side of that mark. Hence, as that mark begins to have a required side only when a yacht starts, if that mark is not more than one boat's length from the starting line when she starts, her wake will not lie on the required side of that mark and she will infringe rule 51.2.

Curiously enough, in 1977, 45 years after the

Royal Corinthian YC submitted the first appeal on this situation, the similar case of *Morning Cloud* v *Marionette, Loujaine, Winsome 77, Knockout, Yeoman XX* and *Synergy*, occurred under the burgee of the same club during Cowes Week. In all fairness, it must be stressed that the race committee was not at fault, as the Cowes Combined Clubs' sailing instructions specified the layout of the starting line, and the race committee could not move the South Bramble buoy which served as the outer limit mark of the starting line, while the protest committee was in no doubt about dismissing *Morning Cloud's* protest.

Sailing Instruction 9, Starting Line, read:

'A. The Starting Line is formed by bringing the RYS Flagstaff into line with the orange diamond on the roof of the Castle.

'B. The outer limit mark of the Starting Line will be either to the South Bramble Buoy or the West Bramble Buoy nearer to the Starting Line transit.

'C. The inner limit of the Starting Line will be a Crewsaver buoy. For the purpose of IYRU rule 42.3, both outer and inner limit marks are marks of the Starting Line. Yachts must start by crossing the Starting Line between these two marks.'

*Morning Cloud* protested under SIs 9B, 9C and the paragraph following alleging that the above-listed yachts started to the north of the OLM and did not cross the starting line between the outer and inner limit marks as specifically prescribed in the SIs. The protest committee found that both the inner and outer limit marks were on the pre-start side of the Starting Line transit defined in SI 9A; that all six protested yachts, between the preparatory and starting signals, passed between the outer and inner limit marks and did not cross the starting line until after the starting signal had been made—they started in the same way as did A in Fig. 41 and that they complied with the SIs. It dismissed the protest, and *Morning Cloud* appealed on the grounds that have already been discussed. The Council dismissed the appeal on the facts found and for the reasons given by the protest committee. The Council pointed out that the reference in the

SIs to rule 42.3 was incorrect: it should be rule 42.4.

It is interesting to record that Major Peter Snowden, secretary to the Cowes Combined Clubs, told me subsequently that the Spanker Buoy, then between the West and South Bramble Buoys was to be moved with the intention of overcoming the disadvantages of the existing starting line when starting to the westward.

## Touching a Starting Mark

The following problem was posed by the secretary of the Wood Spring Model Yacht Club:

*Problem.* 'We use a one-minute countdown to the start (usually broadcast with a cassette-type recorder). During this period, but well before the starting signal, a boat is crossing the starting line from the course side and, through lack of attention, runs over a starting mark (Fig. 42). She rounded the mark immediately and then made a normal start without suffering any disadvantage. It is believed that the rounding should have been carried out after the starting signal and after starting, but before setting course for the first mark. In this case the manoeuvre would certainly be a disadvantage, but seems unfair since the contact with the mark could not affect the outcome of the race.

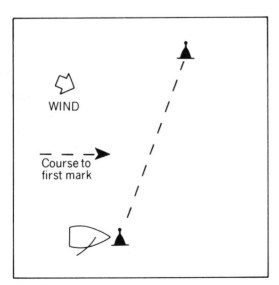

**Fig. 42**

'Under rule 51.3, the starting mark does not have a required side before a yacht starts, but this is not the same as saying it may be ignored. Rule 52.1 refers to 'a starting mark before starting' but does not seem to deal with the period of time well before the starting signal is made.'

*Answer.* 'A yacht that touches a starting mark at any time between her preparatory and starting signals infringes rule 52.1(a)(i), the reason being that the preamble to Part V, which includes rule 52, states:

> a yacht is subject to the rules of Part V only when she is *racing*.

'The term *racing* is defined in Part 1—Definitions, as:

> *Racing*—A yacht is *racing* from her preparatory signal until she has *finished*. . .

'The penalty for touching a starting mark during the period between the preparatory and starting signals is laid down in rule 52.2(b)(i), which states:

> (b) When a yacht touches: (i) a starting *mark*, she shall carry out the rounding after she has *started*. . .

and the rounding penalty manoeuvre itself is described in rule 52.2(a).

'The definition of starting reads:

> A yacht *starts* when, after fulfilling her penalty obligations, if any . . , and after her starting signal, any part of her hull, crew or equipment first crosses the starting line in the direction of the course to the first *mark*.

'Thus, a careful reading of the relevant rules and definitions reveals that the boat did not make a legal start.

'With regard to the question of fairness, until the principle of the present rule 52.2 was introduced in 1969, experienced yachtsmen regarded the proper rounding of a mark as an essential test of good helmsmanship so, to drive home this lesson, hitting it was penalised by retirement or disqualification.'

When I published this problem as an article in a yachting magazine, the explanation was queried by a reader, who commented as follows:

'In your article, you quote from the rules as follows: "When a yacht touches a starting *mark*, she shall carry out the rounding after she has *started*." (This is 52.2(b)(i)—author) And again: "*Starting*—A yacht *starts* when, after fulfilling her penalty obligations . . ., any part of her hull . . . first crosses the starting line." (This is a definition—author). Perhaps my efforts at programming computers have made me somewhat over-literal, but this does seem to present an impossibility.'

My answer was that the starting definition was introduced in 1961, while rule 52.2(b)(i) arrived in 1973. As far as I was aware, no one had previously suggested that there was any conflict between the definition and the rule, nor had any appeal arisen on the subject. I thus considered that my correspondent had misdirected himself by incorrectly quoting the definition but, before commenting on his stricture, I sought the opinion of the IYRU Racing Rules Committee chairman, Lynn Watters, who replied as follows:

'The way I read the definition of starting is different, thus: "*Starting*—A yacht *starts* when, after fulfilling her penalty obligations . . . under rule 51.1(c) . . ., any part of her hull . . . first crosses the starting line . . ." This makes no reference to the penalty obligation under rule 52.2(b)(i), only to the one under rule 51.1(c), so she would therefore have to start correctly without infringing rule 51.1(c) before she carried out any penalty rounding under rule 52.2(b)(i). I do not see that there is any conflict. Have I missed something?'.

I was relieved to have my explanation endorsed in this way. Rule 51.1(c) refers to the so-called One-Minute Rule after a General Recall.

## Are We Over?

No matter how a rule is worded, race officers and helmsmen can misconstrue it. In the appeal of *Polly* v Race Committee (RYA 1981/4) the facts were that *Polly* approached the starting line from its course side, and she was still about 20 yards on that side of it when the starting signal was made. She then luffed up and proceeded to race. At no time had she been on the pre-start side of the starting line.

The race officer therefore considered her to be a non-starter, on the grounds that neither rule 8.2 (Recalls), nor rule 50 (Ranking as a Starter), applied. In fact, when rule 8.2 is read carefully, it should be obvious that it could never be so interpreted. *Polly* sought redress from the race committee under what is now rule 69 (Requests for Redress), because she was not recalled, no recall signals having been made.

Rules 8.2(a) and 8.2(b) use the phrase, 'has wholly returned to the pre-start side of the line'. The race officer argued that the significant word is 'returned', and that a yacht in *Polly's* position could not return to a point on the pre-start side of the line that she had not previously occupied.

Although this argument is logical, as far back as 1908, the then rule 28—Recalls, stated in part:

> If any Yacht, or any part of her hull, spars or other equipment be on or across the starting line when the signal to start is made, her recall number shall be displayed as soon as possible, and a suitable sound signal also given to call the attention of the competitors to the fact that a recall number is being displayed. The Yacht recalled must return and re-cross the line to the satisfaction of the Committee . . .

Thus the intention of the rule has always been to regard any yacht that is on the course side of the starting line when the starting signal is made as a premature starter and subject to a recall. It is interesting to note that, prior to the race committee's reference of this case to the RYA, the rule's intention had never been queried.

The present rule 51.1(b) (Sailing the Course, reads:

> Unless otherwise prescribed in the sailing instructions, a yacht which either crosses pre-

**Plate 16**   Are we over? Where a starting line has a mark only at each end (i.e. there is no transit or range) as at this 1980 Fireball European Championship race, good judgement is important.          *Colin Jarman*

maturely, or is on the course side of the starting line or its extensions, at the starting signal, shall return and *start* in accordance with the definition.

The Council's decision in this case was: 'The race committee's decision to uphold *Polly's* request for redress is confirmed.

'As, at her starting signal, *Polly's* hull, crew and equipment were on the course side of the starting line, rules 8.2(b) (Recalls), 51.1(a) and 51.1(b) (Sailing the Course), applied. The fact that *Polly* had not been on the pre-start side of the starting line does not nullify rule 51.1(b).

'As *Polly* did not cross the starting line to its pre-start side and start in accordance with the definition of starting, she did not start. Nevertheless, for the purpose of scoring points and

awarding prizes, she ranked as a starter in accordance with rule 50 (Ranking as a Starter). However, as at the starting signal the race committee apparently did not lower the class flag to 'the dip' and make a sound signal, *Polly* may have been misled into believing she had started. Consequently, she was entitled to seek redress from the race committee under what is now rule 69 (Requests for Redress).

'It is for the race committee, being aware of the local conditions, to decide when a yacht is in the vicinity of the starting line and therefore entitled to be recalled. The case of *Maia* v Royal Gourock Yacht Club (YRA 1952/8) refers.

'In the case of *Persephone* v Royal Torbay Yacht Club (YRA 1950/9), it was ruled that the removal of a recall number before the recalled yacht had returned to the pre-start side of the starting line justified her in believing that the number had been displayed in error, and that she was not subject to recall.

'However, when a yacht is aware that she is on the course side of the starting line at the start and that she has not returned across it, she is not entitled to continue racing.'

## Questions
**Q6.1**   When does a yacht start?

**Q6.2**   The starting signal is given at L1W1, while W is still clear astern of L. May L luff as she pleases at L2W2, which is ten seconds after the starting signal and before W has L's Mast Abeam?

**Q6.3**   In the start shown in question 6.2, W establishes Mast Abeam at L3W3, but loses it again before either yacht reaches the starting line, though the overlap is not broken. May L luff at L4W4?

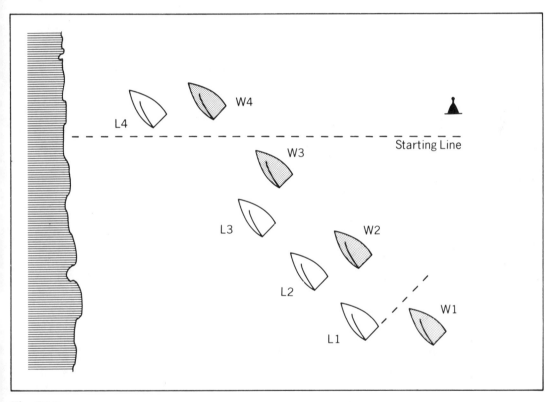

**Fig. Q6.2**

# 7 Rounding or Passing Marks and Obstructions

There are more protests and appeals relating to rule 42 (Rounding or Passing Marks and Obstructions) than to any other rule in the book, and the first main reason is that many helmsmen fail to understand that rule 42 is in Section C of Part IV—Rules which Apply at Marks and Obstructions and other Exceptions to the Rules of Section B, (which consists of Principal Right-of-Way Rules and their Limitations). Helmsmen would save themselves a great deal of misunderstanding, argument and ill-feeling if they would always bear in mind the fact that rule 42 makes exception to the Opposite Tacks—Basic Rule 36, the Same Tack—Basic Rule 37 and the Changing Tacks—Tacking and Gybing Rule 41, only when in the interests of both safety and equity it is essential to do so.

The second main reason is that, as each mark in the course is a focal point on which all the yachts converge, the area in its immediate vicinity inevitably tends to become congested, and the risk of collisions between yachts is greatly increased.

The third main reason is that many helmsmen do not exercise intelligent anticipation. They fail to appreciate the fact that, if they hold their course and do not take any avoiding action required by the rules while they have the room and opportunity to do so, they will often become involved in collisions and protests, and subject to possible disqualification or some other penalty.

Rule 42 is divided into four sections headed, 42.1 Room at Marks and Obstructions when Overlapped; 42.2 Clear Astern and Clear Ahead in the Vicinity of Marks and Obstructions; 42.3 Limitations on Establishing and Maintaining an Overlap in the Vicinity of Marks and Obstructions; and 42.4 At a Starting Mark Surrounded by Navigable Water. This section deals with rule 42.1.

However, to comprehend the operation of rule 42 as a whole, it is necessary to mention some associated points. First, throughout rule 42 the words rounding and passing are used. It was ruled in the case of *Alouette* v Zanzibar Sailing Club (RYA 1951/14) that:

The distinction between rounding and passing a mark lies in the fact that a mark can be rounded only when it entails a substantial alteration of course, whereas a mark may be passed without any alteration of course.

In accordance with rule 51.2 (Sailing the Course), when rounding a mark, a string representing a yacht's course when drawn taut must bear on the mark, whereas when passing a mark, the string need not do so. The words 'need not' are used advisedly, for a reason that is obvious when there are three successive marks nearly in a straight line, the middle one having to be passed on the same side as the other two. For example, the windward mark of a triangular course can only be rounded by altering course; but when the sailing instructions prescribe that certain channel marks must be passed on their deep-water sides, no alteration of course may be necessary.

## Overlap

The next point concerns the definitions:

*Clear Astern* and *Clear Ahead: Overlap*—A yacht is *clear astern* of another when her hull and equipment in

66

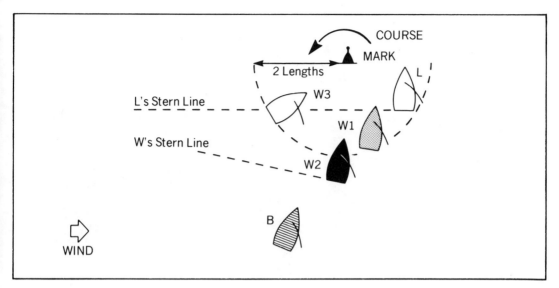

**Fig. 43**

normal position are abaft an imaginary line projected abeam from the aftermost point of the other's hull and equipment in normal position. The other yacht is *clear ahead.*

The yachts *overlap* when neither is *clear astern*; or when, although one is *clear astern,* an intervening yacht *overlaps* both of them.

The terms *clear astern, clear ahead* and *overlap* apply to yachts on opposite *tacks* only when they are subject to rule 42, (Rounding or Passing Marks and Obstructions).

Fig. 43 illustrates these definitions. By taking the stern line of L, it will be seen that W2 is clear astern of her and that she is clear ahead of W2. However, W1 overlaps L and therefore is not clear astern of her. Similarly, W2 overlaps W1 and as W1 overlaps both L and W2, W1 ranks as an intervening yacht, consequently L and W2 overlap. W3, although converging on L, W1 and W2, overlaps all three. B is clear astern of W2, W1 and L, and under rule 37.2 must keep clear of them. Note that the term intervening clearly implies that, for W1 to rank as an intervening yacht, she must be between L and W2.

The phrase 'equipment in normal position' is used in the above definition to prevent a yacht clear astern claiming to have established an overlap on a yacht clear ahead by, for

example, deliberately easing her spinnaker sheet and guy, and allowing the sail to blow out forward of its normal position.

Rule 42.1(a) reads:

42.1    ROOM AT MARKS AND OBSTRUCTIONS WHEN OVERLAPPED
When yachts are about to round or pass a *mark,* other than a starting *mark* surrounded by navigable water, on the same required side or an *obstruction* on the same side:

(a) An outside yacht shall give each yacht *overlapping* her on the inside, room to round or pass the *mark* or *obstruction,* except as provided in rules 42.1(c), 42.1(d) and 42.4, (At a Starting Mark Surrounded by Navigable Water).
Room includes room for an *overlapping* yacht to *tack* or *gybe* when either is an integral part of the rounding or passing manoeuvre.

There are two important points here. First, when the starting line is laid in accordance with rule 6(c) (Starting and Finishing Lines), the shore end of which is denoted by two beacons or posts in transit, rule 42.1(a) applies at that end, but not to the outer end when it is denoted by a mark surrounded by navigable water.

**Plate 17**   If Mirror 50144 maintains her leeward overlap on 39292, she will be third round the next port-hand mark, because rule 42.1(a) requires the latter to give each yacht overlapping her on the inside, room to round or pass the mark.
*Arthur Sidey*

Secondly, IYRU Interpretations, Case 40, states:

The word 'room' in rule 42.1(a) means the space needed by an inside yacht, which, in the prevailing conditions is handled in a seamanlike manner, to pass in safety between an outside yacht and the *mark* or *obstruction*.

This means that the inside yacht is not entitled to claim the room that she would consider technically desirable, in order to make an ideal rounding of the mark in the absence of the outside yacht. The room needed would be enough clearance on both sides to allow for some error of judgement or execution, but with the outside yacht entitled to force the inside yacht to make a somewhat sharper than normal rounding.

Figure 44(a) shows a situation in which two close-hauled port-tack overlapping yachts, L and W, are within two lengths of a windward mark at which tacking is an integral part of rounding it. Before rounding the mark, L held right of way under rule 37.1, but now, as the outside yacht under rule 42.1(a), she is required to give W, the inside yacht, room to tack to round the mark. If, in tacking, W's quarter swings out and touches L, L will have infringed rule 42.1(a).

Similarly, Fig. 44(b) shows two starboard-tack overlapping yachts gybing as an integral part of rounding a mark. Here, the inside yacht, L, holds right of way as the leeward yacht under rule 37.1, so W, as the windward outside yacht must not only keep clear of L, but she must also take care that she is not so close to L that L's boom as it gybes touches any part of W's hull or equipment, otherwise W will have infringed rules 37.1 and 42.1(a).

Rule 42.1(b) reads:

> (b) When an inside yacht of two or more *overlapped* yachts either on opposite *tacks*, or on the same *tack* without *luffing* rights, will have to *gybe* in order most directly to assume a *proper course* to the next *mark*, she shall *gybe* at the first reasonable opportunity.

Figure 45 shows P and S running on opposite tacks to a leeward port-handed mark around which S will have to gybe. Rule 42.1(b) requires S, although holding right of way under rule 36, to gybe and assume her proper course to the next mark at the first reasonable opportunity.

In this connection, it is important to remember that when two yachts gybe as shown in Fig. 44(b), and one yacht gybes as shown in Fig. 45, in both cases when the outside yacht becomes the leeward yacht, even though she may not have luffing rights after the gybe has been completed, she is entitled to luff up to her proper course and the windward yacht must keep clear.

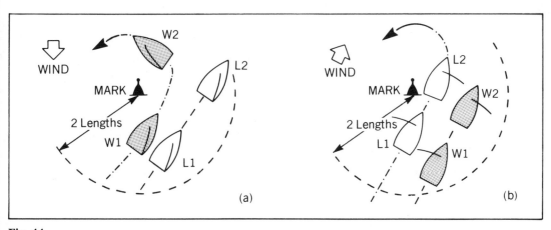

**Fig. 44**

**Plate 18**    The opportunity for incidents – or even outright chaos – is increased as the fleet converges on each mark in turn. A sound knowledge of rule 42 (Rounding or Passing Marks and Obstructions) is required if situations such as this are to be avoided – or capitalised on.

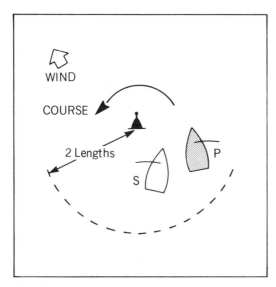

**Fig. 45**

In the case of USYRU Appeal No. 12, 1941, L and W were running on starboard tack to a starboard-hand leeward mark, around which they had to luff on to a close-hauled course. In so doing, as a result of poor seamanship, W, the inside yacht, failed to luff up to her proper course. L continued to give way to avoid contact until the yachts were three lengths from and past the mark, when the yachts touched, beam to beam, without damage.

It was ruled that W infringed rule 37.1 in failing to keep clear of L who, even though she did not have luffing rights, was entitled to sail up to her proper course. The room to which W was entitled was only that sufficient in the circumstances to round safely and clear the mark.

Rule 42.1(b) is one example of the IYRU RRC's intention to try to ensure that yachts sail the course and round its marks with the minimum amount of mutual interference and 'bloody-mindedness'. It is also a safety measure.

When in Fig. 45 a number of other port-tack yachts are overlapping P to leeward of her and are waiting for her to luff round the mark, it prohibits S from insisting on her starboard-tack rights, holding her course, forcing all the port-tack yachts to gybe and generally creating chaos before finally gybing herself and rounding the mark.

Figure 46 shows two close-hauled starboard-tack yachts, L and W, approaching a windward port-handed mark, around which they will have to gybe. Again, the inside yacht, L, holds right of way, this time under rule 37.1, but as she is without luffing rights, she must bear away round the mark and gybe at the first reasonable opportunity, for the same reasons as those in the previous situation.

On the other hand, rule 42.1(b) does not apply to L in Figs. 44(b) and 46 when she holds luffing rights over W. L is then entitled to hold her course or luff and sail W past the mark. This well-known tactic is commonly called reaching a vessel past a mark, and is used sometimes by L in team racing, when W is in the opposing team, but it is a tactic that seldom pays in conventional racing.

Figure 47 shows two close-hauled yachts on opposite tacks, P and S. Although neither is clear astern of the other, and hence by definition they are overlapped, and P is the inside yacht with regard to the mark, the definition also states that the term overlap applies to yachts on opposite tacks only when they are subject to rule 42, and rule 42.1(c) quoted above says that in such circumstances rule 42.1(a) shall not apply. Consequently, in the situation shown in Fig. 47 P must bear away, pass under S's stern and then tack to round the mark.

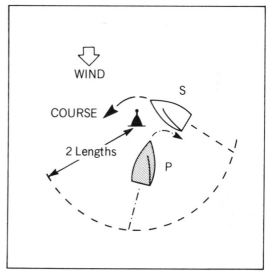

**Fig. 47**

Rule 42.1(c) also applies in two variations of the above situation. It exempts from the two-lengths determinative of rule 42.3(a)(ii) all situations in which one or both close-hauled yachts will have to tack close to the windward mark in order to round it. It should be noted that rule 42.1(a)(ii) applies only to establishing a late inside overlap from clear astern, a situation that rarely happens in the conditions being discussed. This rule will be dealt with in due course.

The principle of rule 42.1(c) was introduced in 1969—but its original number and wording have since been changed—as a result of the following question submitted by the RYA to the IYRU RRC in 1967, that arose from the

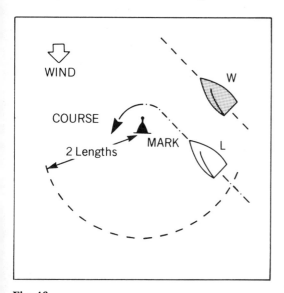

**Fig. 46**

## Opposite Tacks

Rule 42.1(c) reads:

> (c) When two yachts on opposite *tacks* are on a beat or when one of them will have to *tack* either to round the *mark* or to avoid the *obstruction*, as between each other, rule 42.1(a) shall not apply and they are subject to rules 36, (Opposite Tacks—Basic Rule), and 41 (Changing Tacks—Tacking and Gybing).

case of *Sano-y-Salvo* v *Zipidi* (RYA 1968/9) and is shown in Fig. 48.

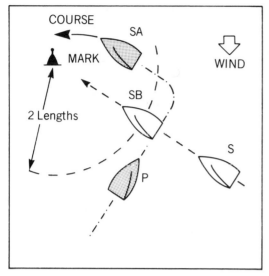

**Fig. 48**

When P crosses S, which is fetching a windward port-hand mark, and P completes a tack to starboard to windward of S's course just within two lengths of the mark and becomes SA, with SB only a few feet clear astern of SA, SB has scarcely anywhere to go. Rule 41 has not been infringed, since P cleared S's course before tacking, but owing to SA's proximity SB can luff to windward of SA only with great difficulty, and unless SB can get room from SA, SB's only alternative is to bear away and pass to leeward of the mark. What are the rights and obligations of SA and SB in this situation?

The IYRU RRC decided that some change in the rules was needed, meanwhile the position was that: 'When in the situation described, P completes a tack so close to windward of S that SB has no alternative but to establish an inside overlap on SA, SA should give SB room to round or pass the mark on the required side.'

Rules 42.1(c) and 42.3(a)(ii) were amended to give effect to this decision. It entitles the inside yacht, SB, to room at the mark unless S—rather than the outside yacht, SA, by the act of tacking—establishes her overlap so late

that the outside yacht is unable to give room. (Rule 42.3(a)(i)).

Turning now to the situation shown in Fig. 49, suppose P argues that rule 42.1(c) entitles her to tack between S and the mark when they are within two lengths of it, and then claims room at the mark under rule 42.1(a). Note first that the two-lengths determinative does not apply. Secondly as, upon completing her tack, P becomes the leeward yacht, and as neither yacht has been clear astern of the other, rule 42.3(a)(ii) does not apply. By removing the two-lengths determinative from the application of rule 42.1(c), which refers to yachts, 'one of them will have to tack . . . to round the mark', this becomes a same-tack situation. Thirdly, the rule says nothing about tacking between another yacht and a mark. Consequently, either rule 37.1 or rule 42.1(a) applies and, as they mutually reinforce each other, in most cases a protest committee can proceed under either, with perhaps a preference for the basic rule.

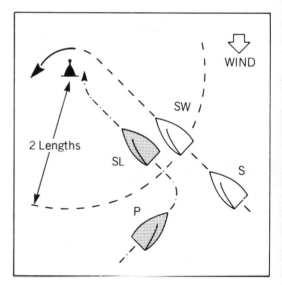

**Fig. 49**

Even if, after SL had completed her tack to starboard she were abaft the Mast Abeam position and had no luffing rights, she is entitled to sail up to her proper course, which in some cases would enable her to luff above a close-hauled course and 'shoot' for the mark, on the grounds that in the absence of SW that would have been her proper course in accordance with the definition.

Figures 48 and 49 both show the two-lengths radius, merely to indicate where in relation to the mark these situations may occur, but it has no bearing on the application of the rules to them. It is also assumed that in all cases the tacking yacht has complied with rule 41.

## Luffing

We now come to rule 42.1(d), which reads:

> (d) An outside *leeward yacht* with luffing rights may take an inside yacht to windward of a *mark* provided that she hails to that effect and begins to *luff* before she is within two of her overall lengths of the *mark* and provided that she also passes to windward of it.

Figure 50 shows two overlapping port-tack yachts on a reach, L and W, approaching a port-hand mark. When L has luffing rights she can exercise them as she pleases, except that she cannot luff W into any kind of danger, and she can luff W to windward, or to the wrong side, of the mark, subject to rule 42.1(d). L cannot luff W to windward of the mark and then at the last moment bear away and round or pass it on the right or required side herself. If L wants to try to break the overlap before she reaches the mark, she must observe rule 42.1(d) and begin to luff before she is within two lengths of the mark.

It was ruled in the case of *Jerry Pip* v *Teal* (RYA 1972/6; IYRU Case 60) that:

A leeward yacht with luffing rights is required to hail (under rule 42.1(d)) only when she intends to luff when 'about to round a mark'. There is no such requirement in open water.

With regard to the interpretation of the phrase 'about to round', the decision of

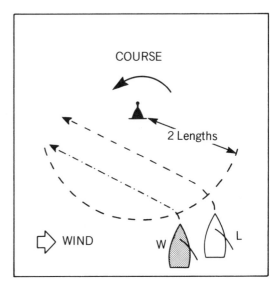

**Fig. 50**

USYRU Appeal No. 145, 1971, gives some helpful guidance:

> 'When does a yacht become about to round a mark, has been a perennial question although not one which has caused real complications by not being answered by a precise determination. Clearly, a yacht two lengths from a mark and steering a course to round it on the required side is "about to round" it within the meaning of rule 42, and this could be true at a somewhat greater distance as well. Equally clearly, a yacht a quarter-of-a-mile from a mark is not "about to round" it. In approaching a mark there is no exact point at which a yacht becomes a yacht "about to round". The distance varies, too, with such factors as the speed of the yachts, the size of the yachts, the amount of sail handling to be carried out just before or after rounding. In any event, the transition is gradual, the nearer a yacht is to a mark, the more definitely she is about to round it, the more she is committed to do so, the more her competitors expect her to do so, and plan their own courses accordingly, and the more she is obligated to give clear notice if she is planning to luff in accordance with rule 42.1(d).
>
> 'This may seem like begging the question, but it is to be noted that Rule 42 has a good many provisions and they do not all apply at the same distance from a mark. The two-lengths determinative establishes the distance at which an inside overlap must be in effect in order to entitle the inside yacht to room under

rule 42.1(a). The room, however, will be given later and may not even be started to be allowed for until later. If a yacht wishes to take another yacht the wrong side of the mark she must start her manoeuvre before coming within two lengths of the mark.

'The important thing to keep in mind is that the rights and obligations of Rule 42 are designed to bring about a consistent rounding with equity to all yachts concerned, and when such a rounding is made problems do not arise.

'In the present case, Rule 42.1(d) was not involved since L did not take W to windward of the mark. L employed the well-known tactic of luffing and subsequently bearing away in a successful attempt to be clear ahead when she came within two lengths of the mark. At six lengths from a mark in a moderate breeze a dinghy is not "about to round" a mark within the meaning of Rule 42. Therefore, L was entitled by Rule 38 to luff as she pleased.'

## Clear Astern and Clear Ahead

The question of clear astern and clear ahead is governed by rule 42.2, which reads:

42.2   CLEAR ASTERN AND CLEAR AHEAD IN THE VICIN-
       ITY OF MARKS AND OBSTRUCTIONS
       When yachts are about to round or pass a *mark*, other than a starting *mark* surrounded by navigable water, on the same required side or an *obstruction* on the same side:

       (a) A yacht *clear astern* shall keep clear in anticipation of and during the rounding or passing manoeuvre when the yacht *clear ahead* remains on the same *tack* or *gybes*.

       (b) A yacht *clear ahead* which *tacks* to round a *mark* is subject to rule 41, (Changing Tacks—Tacking and Gybing), but a yacht *clear astern* shall not *luff* above *close-hauled* so as to prevent the yacht *clear ahead* from *tacking*.

The combined effect of these two rules is, on the one hand, to control the manoeuvres of the yacht clear astern and, on the other hand, to point out to the yacht clear ahead that, although she is allowed to round a mark by luffing or gybing without regard to the yacht clear astern, she is not allowed to round it by tacking, unless she can comply with rule 41

and thereafter, when applicable, with the Opposite Tacks—Basic Rule 36.

When, in 1876, the Yacht Racing Association first formulated its rules they were based on the International Regulations then generally known as the Board of Trade Rules. Consequently, the YRA rules used the terms 'an overtaking' and 'an overtaken' yacht and required the former to keep clear of the latter.

When the IYRU adopted its first universally-approved rules in 1961, although the above basic principle was (and still is) retained, the original terms were deleted in favour of 'clear astern' and 'clear ahead', which have been explained; see Fig. 43.

This change resulted from the substitution of the American right-of-way rules originated by Harold S. Vanderbilt which, among other features, eliminated the vexatious and conflicting differences between the rights and obligations of a leeward overtaking and a leeward converging yacht *vis-à-vis* a windward yacht. Since that date, the terms 'overtaking' and 'overtaken' yachts have no longer appeared in the rules.

Rule 42.2(a) protects the right of a yacht clear ahead to round a mark by luffing or gybing—but not by tacking—in the most advantageous way, without interference from the yacht clear astern.

When a leeward mark ends a run and the next leg is a beat—the so-called sausage—it is always preferable that A, the yacht clear ahead in Fig. 51, on her approach to the mark, should keep well away from it, so that, as she hardens her sheets and luffs, she makes a smooth and gradual turn. In so doing, she accelerates, and when abreast of the mark she is close-hauled and as high on the wind as possible at the start of the ensuing beat, A is shown making such a rounding, during which B, the yacht clear astern, must keep clear.

Alternatively, when B steers the course shown, straight for the mark before beginning the recommended rounding, she will end up at position 3, having thrown away some valuable weather gage, while if she makes a sharp turn, she will slow down or even stop.

It is in a situation of this kind that the

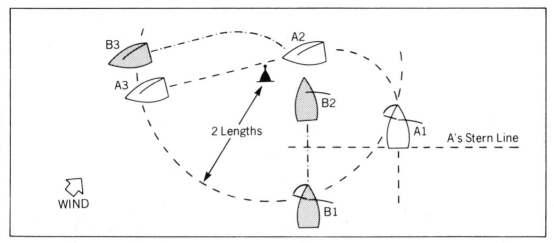

**Fig. 51**

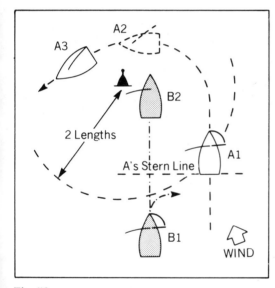

**Fig. 52**

tion of and during A's rounding manoeuvre as she luffs up to a close-hauled course. The fact that when A luffs, her stern line swings aft and causes B to overlap her, is irrelevant, because this happens within two lengths of the mark.

Fig. 52 shows A and B running on starboard tack to a leeward port-hand mark, round which they will have to gybe to assume a close-hauled port-tack course on the ensuing beat. As at position 1, B is clear astern of A when A comes within two lengths of the mark, B must keep clear because the same principles apply. Moreover, should B delay her gybe, as shown at A2B2, she cannot claim starboard-tack rights because rule 42.2(a) makes exception to rule 36. Hence in Figs. 51 and 52, B would be well advised to follow in A's wake round the mark.

The rules have been discussed when gybing round a leeward mark from a run to a beat, but they also apply when gybing round a beam or wing mark from a reach to a reach.

Before leaving this subject, it is worth repeating the ruling in USYRU Appeal No. 38, 1950, in which it was stated:

. . . it is an established principle of yacht racing that when a yacht voluntarily or unintentionally makes room available to another yacht which has no right under the rules to such room, nor makes or indicates any claim to it, such as to pass between her and a mark or obstruction, the other yacht may take advantage, at her own risk, of the room so given.

inexperienced novice steering B often gets into trouble. At position 1, B may mistakenly believe that she has plenty of room to round the mark inside A, only to find at the last moment that A hails, 'You can't come in here'—or words to that effect—and shuts her out, as shown at position 2.

What B must always remember is that at position 1 she is clear astern of A and is required by the Same Tack—Basic Rule 37.2, and by rule 42.2(a), to keep clear in anticipa-

**Plate 19**   K6280 must give room at the mark to K6565, because the latter overlapped inside her before they came within two of K6280's overall lengths of the mark (rule 42.1(a)); this includes room to gybe if that is an integral part of the rounding manoeuvre. Both must keep clear in anticipation of the leading dinghy's rounding manoeuvre when she remains on the same tack or gybes (rule 42.2(a)), because they are clear astern.

Hence, if the other yacht misjudges the amount of room available and touches either the mark, the yacht originally clear ahead, or both, she infringes rules 37.2 and 42.2(a).

Another important point is that rule 42 relates only to yachts that are about to round or pass a mark on the same required side. When, as sometimes happens, yachts round the same mark in opposite directions, rule 36 (Opposite Tacks) and not rule 42 applies.

Such potentially dangerous situations ought never to occur when two classes are racing at the same time under the jurisdiction of the same club. The cases of *Waterwitch* (YRA 1932/ 6); *Howdee Doodee* v *Sooky* (RYA 1968/6; IYRU

Case 37): and *Hellhound* v *Hare* (RYA 1971/4; IYRU Case 51) refer. However in some places more than one club sets courses on the same waters, and un-beknown to one another, the courses they set may require a navigational mark to be rounded in opposite ways.

We now come to rule 42.2(b), which ties in with rule 42.1(c). Fig. 53 shows two close-hauled starboard-tack yachts, A and B, approaching a starboard-hand windward mark around which they will have to tack. A is clear ahead of B and is allowed to tack only when she can first comply with rule 41 and then with rule 36, that is to say, A is far enough ahead of B that A, now P, can complete her

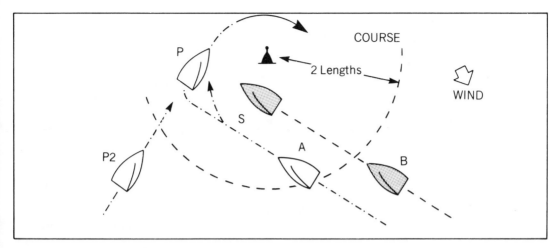

**Fig. 53**

tack to port and cross clear ahead of B, now S. It is in these circumstances that rule 42.2(b) prohibits S from luffing above close-hauled to prevent P from tacking. This situation can be shown in Fig. 53 by assuming that P2 was originally ahead and to leeward of A and had tacked to port and had cleared A. A cannot then luff, as shown by her dotted course, she must hold her close-hauled course, pass astern of P and not try to touch her. This is an opposite-tack situation in which A has no luffing rights, since rule 38.1 (Same Tack—Luffing and Sailing above a Proper Course after Starting), does not apply.

The relationship between B and A also illustrates the time-honoured manoeuvre of reaching a vessel past a mark, referred to earlier. As A cannot tack, she must hold her course, and when B comes abreast of the mark and is in a position to tack to round it, there is no rule that requires her to do so and proper course does not apply. B can therefore hold her course as long as she pleases and can force A to overstand the mark. The case of the Yokohama Yacht Club (RYA 1964/2, IYRU Case 17) refers.

This is a common team racing tactic when B has a team mate, P2. B holds her course, forces A to overstand the mark, lets P2 pass under her stern to round the mark first, then tacks to round the mark in second place, leaving A to tack and follow in third place

When A is not allowed to tack to round the mark it may be asked how, if she cannot tack to round the mark ahead of B, can she round the mark at all? She can do so quite easily as shown in Fig. 54.

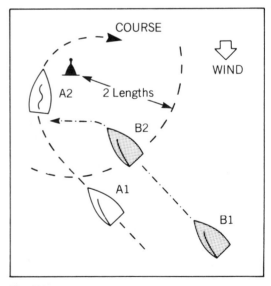

**Fig. 54**

It is important to remember that, by definition, a yacht does not begin the act of tacking until she has passed beyond the head to wind position. Under rule 38.1, A is entitled to luff as she pleases up to head to wind. Consequently, when A is nearly abreast of the mark, instead of putting her helm hard down and tacking contrary to rule 41, she should sail gradually into the wind, remaining on the same tack. Then, as A luffs, B, the yacht clear astern, must keep clear, and as at this late stage she is not entitled to establish an inside overlap on A, her only alternative is to bear away and pass under A's stern, as shown at position 2. As soon as B's bow is abreast of A2's stern, so that B cannot luff, A can then tack to round the mark comfortably without infringing rule 41.

It has been suggested that there is a conflict between rule 35(b)(ii), (Limitations on Altering Course)—which allows a close-hauled, starboard-tack, right-of-way yacht to luff above close hauled when rounding a mark by tacking—and rule 42.2(b) (Clear Astern and Clear Ahead in the Vicinity of Marks and Obstructions) which says:

> . . . a yacht *clear astern* shall not *luff* above *close-hauled* so as to prevent the yacht *clear ahead* from *tacking*.

Rule 42.2(b) was adopted in 1965 to govern what is initially a same-tack situation in which A is clear ahead of B, as in Fig. 53. Hence B is bound by rule 37.2 to keep clear of A; B is not the right-of-way yacht and A has the right, under rule 38.1, to luff as she pleases up to head to wind, and rule 35(a) exempts her from the limitations imposed by rule 35, but A can tack only in compliance with rule 41. It is in this situation that one can mentally take the mark away and judge it as though it happened in open water. Rule 42.2(b) says that when A, in tacking to round the mark, can comply with rule 41, B must not luff above close-hauled to prevent A from tacking, which also applies in open water.

1973 Rule 34(b), (Right-of-Way Yacht Altering Course), did not include what is now rule 35(b)(ii), (Limitations on Altering Course). This rule was designed to govern an opposite-tack situation at a mark. In this case, S is the right-of-way yacht, and her right to luff

under rule 35(b)(ii) applies only when she is rounding the mark. This means that her course to the mark must bring her quite close to it. How close would vary with the conditions, probably not more than a boat's width. At a boat's length or more she would be tacking to get to the mark; not to round it. In such a situation it is obvious that one cannot mentally take the mark away.

Let us now study the opposite-tack relationship between A and P2 in Fig. 53, assuming that B is not there. P2 is bound by rule 36 to keep clear of A. This she can do either by bearing away to pass under A's stern—in which case she will probably be unable to fetch the mark—or by easing sheets, losing way and letting A cross ahead of her, or by tacking and lee-bowing her, when A can again reach P2 past the mark.

## Establishing and Maintaining an Overlap

The first of the previous sections dealt with room at marks and obstructions when overlapped, and we later examined the situation when clear ahead and clear astern in their vicinity. In this look at mark rounding the limitations on establishing and maintaining an overlap are discussed. The relevant rule is 42.3, which appears below.

In the earliest days of yacht racing very few clubs had any rule governing the rounding of marks and obstructions, but when the YRA was drafting its first code of racing rules in 1875 it evidently realised that in the interests of sound seamanship and fair play it was necessary to formulate a rule that controlled the manoeuvres of yachts in these situations. This rule would have to fulfil three somewhat conflicting requirements.

First, when the time came for a yacht clear ahead to round a mark, to protect her rights. Secondly, when the yacht clear ahead was within a short distance of the mark, to warn the yacht clear astern that she must not try to establish a last-minute inside overlap on the yacht clear ahead and thus force a passage. Thirdly, when the yacht clear astern had fairly

**Plate 20** If this mark has to be left to starboard, Mirror 60019 is not obliged to allow 59484 room to tack for it – the latter should have hailed earlier for room to fetch it on her present port tack. If the mark must be left to port, 60019 can hail 59484 for room to lay it only if she established her windward inside overlap outside two of the former's overall lengths of the mark (difficult to judge from this angle, but 60019 went on to win this open meeting from 59484, so perhaps she had). *Arthur Sidey*

established an inside (often windward) overlap on the yacht clear ahead before they reached the mark, to make an exception to what are now the basic opposite-tack and same-tack rules 36 and 37—so as to entitle the inside yacht to claim room to avoid either hitting a mark or running into any kind of danger from which she could not otherwise escape.

It may be of interest and may also help our understanding of the provisions of 1981 IYRU rule 42 to study the very first, 1876, YRA rule on the subject. That read:

20  *Overtaking, rounding marks, etc.* A yacht overtaking another yacht shall keep out of the way of the last-mentioned yacht, but when rounding any buoy or vessel used to mark out the course, should two yachts not be clear of each other at the time the leading yacht is close to, and

actually rounding the mark, the outside yacht must give the other room to pass clear of it, whether it be the lee or weather yacht which is in danger of fouling the mark. No yacht to be considered clear, unless so much ahead as to give a free choice to the other on which side she will pass. An overtaking yacht shall not, however, be justified in attempting to establish an overlap, and thus force a passage between the leading yacht and the mark after the latter yacht has altered her helm for the purpose of rounding.'

The current rule is 42.3 and reads as follows:

42.3  LIMITATIONS ON ESTABLISHING AND MAINTAIN-ING AN OVERLAP IN THE VICINITY OF MARKS AND OBSTRUCTIONS

(a) When a yacht *clear astern* establishes an inside *overlap* she shall be entitled to room under rule 42.1(a), (Room at Marks and

Obstructions when Overlapped), only when the yacht *clear ahead*:

   (i)  is able to give the required room and

  (ii)  is outside two of her overall lengths of the *mark* or *obstruction*, except when one of the yachts has completed a *tack* within two overall lengths of the *mark* or *obstruction*, or when the *obstruction* is a continuing one as provided in rule 42.3(f).

(b)  A yacht *clear ahead* shall be under no obligation to give room to a yacht *clear astern* before an *overlap* is established.

(c)  When an outside yacht is *overlapped* at the time she comes within two of her overall lengths of a *mark* or an *obstruction*, she shall continue to be bound by rule 42.1(a), (Room at Marks and Obstructions when Overlapped), to give room as required even though the *overlap* is thereafter broken.

(d)  A yacht which claims an inside *overlap* has the onus of satisfying the race committee that the *overlap* was established in proper time.

(e)  An outside yacht which claims to have broken an *overlap* has the onus of satisfying the race committee that she became *clear ahead* when she was more than two of her overall lengths from the *mark* or *obstruction*.

(f)  A yacht *clear astern* may establish an *overlap* between the yacht *clear ahead* and a continuing *obstruction*, such as a shoal or the shore or another vessel, only when at that time there is room for her to pass between them in safety.

The commonest cause of trouble is that the yacht clear ahead wants to keep her lead and round the mark first; the yacht clear astern wants to catch her and get the inner berth, thus cutting her out and taking the lead after the mark is rounded.

The yacht clear ahead, perhaps lowering her spinnaker and hauling her sheets, and perhaps gybing, preparatory to rounding the mark, will invariably contend that the yacht coming up from clear astern did not establish the overlap in proper time. The latter, carrying on a few moments longer before hauling sheets and so on, hoping to establish the overlap, will contend that she did establish it in proper time.

Although what is now rule 42 has been

**Plate 21**  K12369 must not force her way into the gap between K11126 and the mark; only if she established her inside overlap while K11126 was outside two of her overall lengths of the mark may she claim room. If the overlap exists as K11126 comes within two of her lengths of the mark, she must give room to the yacht inside her, even though the overlap is thereafter broken. K11126 is under no obligation to give room to a yacht clear astern (rule 42.3), indeed, under those circumstances K12369 would have to keep clear in anticipation of K11126's rounding manoeuvre (rule 42.2).    *Tim Hore*

reworded and amplified from one paragraph to four sections and 13 paragraphs to cover some of the many variables involved, a conversation between two respected members of the yacht racing fraternity of their day, Major Brooke Heckstall-Smith, secretary of the YRA 1898–1944 and Dixon Kemp a leading authority on the sport at the time and the first secretary of the YRA 1875–1898, very many years ago is still pertinent. Heckstall-Smith recounted the conversation in an article in *Yachting World* in 1937.

'More than half a century ago I was sitting on Ryde Pier talking to Dixon Kemp,' he said, 'and I put this case to him just as it is drawn in Fig. 55.

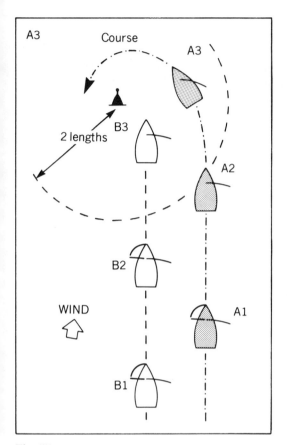

**Fig. 55**

'Let us suppose' I said, 'here are two 20-tonners going to round the mark; there is no overlap at A1B1; there is no overlap at A2B2; a moment later will come A3B3 when, if B hangs on to her spinnaker, or does not haul her boom as soon as A, there will be an overlap. The two crews will never agree as to the exact moment the overlap was made. I know quite well, Mr. Kemp,' I said, 'that in order to claim room, B has got to get the overlap before reaching the mark and before A has altered her helm to round it, and all that stuff in your YRA rules, but, sir, nobody will ever agree as to whether the leading yacht had reached the mark, nor will they agree as to the exact moment she altered her helm; am I not right?'

'Yes,' replied Dixon Kemp, 'You are quite

right on those points; they never did agree and they never will.'

'Then again,' I continued, 'the 20-tonners will have to haul their booms and douse their spinnakers sooner than the 5-tonners, and the twenties much sooner than *Miranda*. How long before she gets to the buoy will *Miranda* have to begin to get in her mainsheet?'

'Quarter-of-a-mile,' said Dixon Kemp, 'More, if she's got a strong fair tide.'

'And when,' I asked, 'would she have to sheet-in if it were a light wind and a foul tide?'

'Not until her bowsprit was past the buoy' he answered.

'That is just my argument, sir,' I went on. 'The rule is so vague; there are dozens, scores of different circumstances; the leading yacht A is the first to deaden her way by hauling sheet and stowing spinnaker; B, the yacht astern, will hang on to her stuff and claim an overlap; nobody, as you say, will ever agree as to the moment when she got her overlap; so which is right?'

'A is right every time', said Dixon Kemp' And don't ever forget it. B should be disqualified for forcing a passage.'

'But should not the rule be altered and made more clear on the point?'

'No,' he said, 'There are 100 points, and whatever you do you cannot work a rule to meet them all; you cannot tell the skipper of the leading yacht when he should haul in his mainsheet, that is his job, and if it's blowing fresh and there's a sea running he must stand by and do so in good time. That is good seamanship. Disqualify the overtaking yacht for forcing a passage; that will teach her skipper not to cut in again.'

That was Dixon Kemp's decision of such cases about a century ago. Since that time the rule has, as we have noted, been expanded but, if we substitute 'clear astern' for 'overtaking' and 'clear ahead' for 'overtaken' and the 'two-lengths determinative', which was introduced in 1965 at the suggestion of Paul Elvström, for that of the phrase 'after the latter yacht has altered her helm for the purpose of rounding', his dictum is still pertinent despite the passage of time.

The importance of the question whether or not overlapped in proper time cannot be minimised, evaded or rejected. It may occur at the last rounding mark, and the result of the race may depend on it. Here it is, win or lose. If the point is disputed by each yacht claiming to be in the right, a collision may be inevitable; a situation which obviously cannot be allowed to continue.

I believe that there is only one seamanlike way to look at this situation. B, as the yacht clear astern, has the basic same-tack rule 37.3 staring her in the face— she must keep clear of A, the yacht clear ahead. Rule 42.3(b) relieves A of any obligation to anticipate that B will establish an inside overlap, so A need do nothing until B actually establishes an overlap. If A then protests against B under rule 42.3(a)(i) or (ii), on the grounds that B did not establish an overlap until A was within two lengths of the mark, B can escape being penalised only by satisfying the protest committee that she discharged the onus placed upon her by rule 42.3(d). In other words, she must convince the protest committee that rule 42.1(a) made an exception to rule 37.2 by relieving her of her obligation to keep clear of A.

Thus, Dixon Kemp's decision given so long ago is still valid—in any case of doubt, B should be disqualified or otherwise penalised; the blame for any accident will lie upon her, the yacht that had been clear astern; she must not risk getting an overlap when there is the smallest doubt, but must go under A's stern and follow in her wake round the mark.

There are two points to note about rule 42.3(a). First, it does not say that B shall not establish an inside overlap—there is no means of preventing her from 'forcing a passage'—but it says that B is entitled to room only when she has established an overlap on A while A is still outside two of her overall lengths of the mark. Secondly, rule 42.3(a) is solely concerned with a yacht establishing an inside overlap from clear astern. Rule 42.3(a)(ii) makes it evident that rule 42.3(a) applies 'except when either yacht has completed a tack within two overall lengths of the mark'. Hence, when two yachts,

P and S, approach a mark close-hauled on opposite tacks, as in Fig. 56(a) and S can fetch the mark, if B can either safely cross ahead of S and tack on S's weather bow, or tack on S's lee bow, as in Fig. 56(b) and establish an overlap within the two-lengths radius of the mark then, as P has never been clear astern of S, rule 42.3(a) does not apply. This exception has already been discussed.

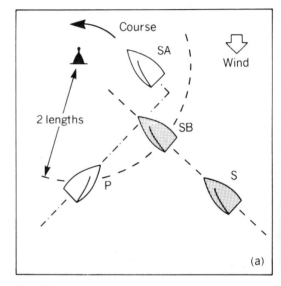

Fig. 56a

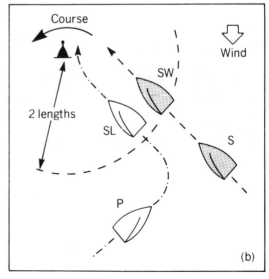

Fig. 56b

Rule 42.3(c) and 42.3(e) should need no elaboration, and rule 42.3(f) will be discussed later.

The racing secretary of the Woodspring Model Sailing Club, raised a problem saying that in most pertinent respects model yacht racing rules are identical with those of the IYRU, one exception being that in rule 42.3(a)(ii) (Rounding or Passing Marks and Obstructions), the determinative is four lengths and not two.

*Problem.* Two model yachts are reaching on starboard tack towards a port-hand gybe mark (see Fig. 57). L has luffing rights. W established an overlap approaching the mark, expecting L to round the mark at the earliest opportunity, but keeping clear with a reasonably generous margin. On reaching the mark, L does not answer her helm and sails on more or less straight for a length and then broaches out of control, contacting W, which is still trying to keep clear, but which is unable to respond quickly enough to L's involuntary manoeuvre. The protest committee found W at fault under rule 37.1, but sympathised with her complaint that it hardly seemed fair. It could not find that L had infringed any rule, but she is well-known for her tendency to broach.

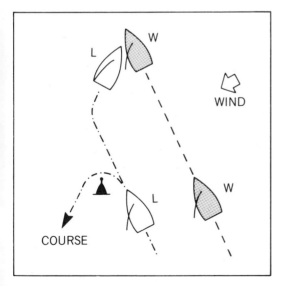

**Fig. 57**

*Answer.* The crucial fact was not found, *viz*, at the moment of contact, did L still have luffing rights? Whereabouts aboard these yachts is the helmsman's normal position? Had these boats been full size, one would be inclined to say that W had not attained the Mast Abeam position. Does W's helmsman ashore hail 'Mast Abeam' to L's helmsman ashore?

If L had luffing rights, and in broaching did not pass beyond head to wind (and the diagram does not suggest that she did) W, in failing to respond to L's sudden luff, infringed rule 37.1.

If L had lost her luffing rights before she broached, she infringed rule 42.1(b), because the course required her to bear away and gybe round the mark at the first reasonable opportunity in order most directly to assume a proper course to the next mark.

## 'Looping' a Mark

It is worth clarifying the two following problems.

*Problem 1.* A yacht in a race sails the intended course for one round, then decides there is a loop in the course and sails this loop on subsequent rounds. She then finishes the course as directed, but the race officer fails to give her a finishing signal. He argues that, as the yacht had not sailed the course, she had not finished. Is the race officer at fault (a) if there is no loop; (b) if there is a loop but the sailing instructions do not cover the point? (Fig. 58 refers.)

*Answer.* (a) When there is no loop. The yacht failed to sail the prescribed course and infringed rule 51.2 (Sailing the Course), but the race officer was wrong in failing to give the yacht a finishing signal. A yacht can be disqualified without a hearing only when she fails either to start or finish correctly. 1981 rule 70.1(a) (Action by Race or Protest Committee) refers. (b) When there is a loop. The sailing instructions must be so worded as to admit of no misunderstanding. The cases of *Bordeaux No. 29*

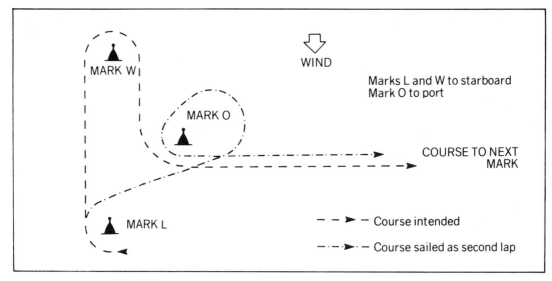

**Fig. 58**

v *Bordeaux No. 28* (RYA 1949/1) and the Karachi Yacht Club (YRA 1954/24) refer. When a reasonable doubt exists about an interpretation of a sailing instruction, the doubt must be resolved in favour of the competitor. USYRU Appeal No. 66 also refers.

*Problem 2.* Windward yacht W approaches a mark, to be left to starboard, on a beam reach and before coming within two lengths of the mark hails for water on a leeward yacht, L (see Fig. 59). L, sailing close-hauled on the same tack, initially ahead of the mast abeam position on W, and for whom the mark is not a mark of the course, hails simultaneously that she is close-hauled. By the time each hail is completed both are within two lengths of the mark. Which rule applies?

*Answer.* The racing rules apply to L and W whether they are competing in the same race or in different races (see Preamble to Part IV).

Assuming for the moment that the mark was a large navigational buoy and L and W were 12ft dinghies, although the buoy would not rank as a mark to L it would rank as an obstruction. If L intended to pass to leeward of it, as W had established an inside overlap on L, under rule 42.1(a) L would be required to

give W room to pass it on the same side. If the mark were a small buoy, as a matter of courtesy and good sportsmanship L should give W room to round the mark. However, in accordance with the strict letter of the law, it could be argued that under the Same Tack—Basic rule 37.1, W should keep clear, either by easing sheets, losing way and letting L pass ahead of her, or by bearing away astern of L and then luffing to round the mark, but there is no case law on this situation.

## A Continuing Obstruction

Helmsmen who race at sea on courses that run along the shore, and on estuaries and rivers along their banks, sometimes find themselves in situations where they are uncertain which rule applies, but before discussing them certain points must be borne in mind. The first concerns good seamanship and always applies, namely, that the rules of Part IV—Right of Way Rules, are framed to enable yachts to compete at close quarters with one another in safety, and therefore prohibit any yacht from deliberately forcing another into any kind of danger. Occasionally a helmsman is heard to hail another: 'If you come in there, I'll luff you

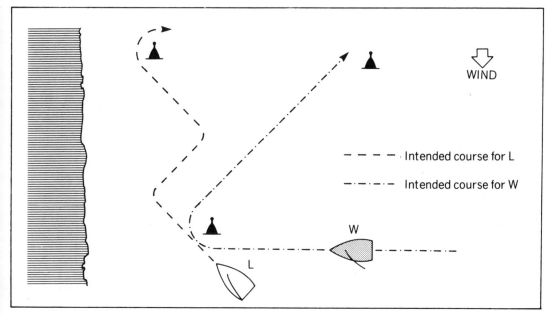

**Fig. 59**

ashore!' That's all bluff and nonsense; see (5) below.

Rule 1 of the YRA from 1876 to 1907, and then rule 1 of the IYRU from 1908 to 1960, read in part:

> ... but as no rules can be devised capable of meeting every incident and accident of sailing, the sailing committee shall keep in view *the ordinary customs of the sea* (my italics) and discourage all attempts to win a race by other means than fair sailing and superior speed and skill.

and although the italicised phrase no longer appears in the Fundamental Rule—Fair Sailing, it is not a 'custom of the sea' for one vessel deliberately to imperil another, and the rules forbid any such dangerous manoeuvres.

The second point is that a yacht clear ahead, A1 or A2 in Fig. 60, can sail as close to either a windward or leeward shore as she deems prudent and, while she is so doing, the yacht clear astern, B1 or B2, is bound to keep clear; see (1) and (2) below.

It has long been held, especially when cheating a foul current, that it would be very unfair

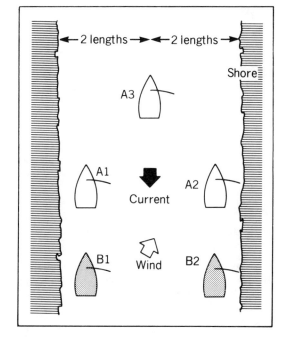

**Fig. 60**

if B1 or B2 in Fig. 61, having perhaps blanketed and closed up on A1 or A2, were entitled to force A1 or A2 to go out into the stronger current to give B1 or B2 room to take advan-

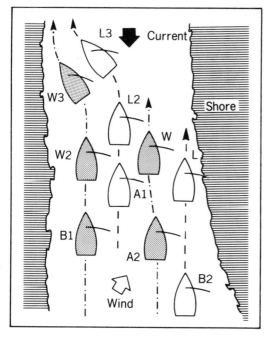

**Fig. 61**

tage of the slacker water near the shore and possibly pass A1 or A2. In this connection, apart from rule 37.2 saying: 'A yacht *clear astern* shall keep clear of a yacht *clear ahead*,' 1981 rule 42.3(f) reads:

> A yacht *clear astern* may establish an *overlap* between the yacht *clear ahead* and a continuing *obstruction*, such as a shoal or the shore or another vessel, only when at that time there is room for her to pass between them in safety.

The expression 'continuing *obstruction*' also includes a pier and a line of anchored vessels, while the phrase 'pass between them in safety' means without touching the yacht that had been clear ahead, or without running aground. In any other circumstances, the yacht that had been clear astern is forcing a passage and does so at her own risk.

Note, too, that rule 42.3(a)(ii) specifically excludes the application of the two-lengths determinative to such situations. The reason is that when yachts are racing in a waterway, the width of which does not exceed four lengths of the yacht clear ahead (A3 in Fig. 60) plus her maximum beam, if she sails in the middle of

the waterway, the application of the two-lengths determinative would prohibit the yachts clear astern (B1 or B3) from trying to pass either to windward or to leeward.

It may be of interest to record that although the above principle has featured in the YRA and IYRU rules since 1876, I have an ancient undated copy of *The Rules and Regulations of the Yare Sailing Club*, in East Anglia, one of which had precisely the opposite effect. Perhaps it is an example of the Norfolk propensity to 'du different'! The club was founded in 1869, i.e., before the YRA; it first appears in the list of recognised yacht clubs in the 1901 YRA yearbook; and was renamed the Yare and Bure Sailing Club in 1911. In 1938 it amalgamated with the Great Yarmouth Yacht Club, the Horning Town Sailing Club and the Norfolk Dinghy Club to form the Norfolk Broads Yacht Club. The rule in question read:

**20**  A boat overhauling another may pass to windward or leeward, and when near the shore or shallow water, or when rounding any mark, flag, or buoy, if the bowsprit or stem of the boat astern overlap any portion of the hull of the boat ahead, the latter must immediately give way and allow the former to pass between her and any such shore, shallow water, mark, flag, or buoy, and should any boat not give way, or compel another to touch the ground or to foul any mark, flag, or buoy, the boat so compelling her shall forfeit all claim to the prize, her owner shall pay all damage that may occur, and the boat so compelled to touch such mark, flag, or buoy, shall not in this case suffer any penalty for such contact.

As a schoolboy, in 1912–1914, I used to crew for M.M.Marshall of Beccles in his Norfolk dinghy *Peggy*, when the above rule was still in force, and I well remember the amount of fierce argument, hard swearing and bad feeling it engendered. I vividly recall racing from Acle to Thurne Mouth, running so close to the bank that *Peggy's* hull was brushing against the reeds, when another dinghy astern forced her stem between *Peggy's* quarter and the bank, loudly hailing for water, which we had to give!

It was not until after World War I had ended and yacht racing was resumed, that this local rule was rescinded and 1920 IYRU rule

31—Giving room at marks or obstructions to sea room, was adopted.

## Summary of Rules Relating to Passing a Continuing Obstruction

1. When a yacht clear ahead, A1 in Fig. 60, is sailing as close to the weather shore as she deems prudent, i.e. just within her draft, the yacht clear astern, B1, may not establish an overlap to windward on A1 and attempt to pass between her and the shore or bank. Same Tack—Basic Rule 37.2 (When not Overlapped); rule 42.2(a) (Clear Astern and Clear Ahead in the Vicinity of Marks and Obstructions); and rule 42.3(f) (Limitations on Establishing and Maintaining an Overlap in the Vicinity of Marks and Obstructions) refer; see also the cases of *Sakuntala* v *Polynia* (YRA 1901/3) and *Thistle* v *Gannet* (RYA 1974/3; IYRU Case 68). The draft of a centreboard yacht is judged as though she were a fixed-keel vessel of draft equal to that of her centreboard at the time in question, provided that it was not lowered farther than a reasonable helmsman would consider seamanlike in all circumstances.

2. When a yacht clear ahead, A2 in Fig. 60, is sailing as close to the lee shore as she deems prudent, the yacht clear astern, B2, may not establish an overlap to leeward on A2 and attempt to pass between her and the shore or bank. The rules quoted in (1) above and the cases of *Sapphire* v *Ruby*; *Ruby* v *Sapphire*, YRA 1924/10, and *Karen* v *Ailsa*, RYA 1962/34, refer.

3. When a yacht clear ahead, A1 in Fig. 61, is not sailing as close to the weather shore as she could, and at that time there is room for the yacht clear astern, B1, to pass between A1 and the shore or bank in safety, B1 can try to establish an inside overlap on A1. Rule 42.3(f) and the cases of *Curacao* v *Petarli II*: *Petarli II* v *Curacao*, (RYA 1967/10); *Bald Eagle* v *Poseidon*, (RYA 1968/11); and the Hunts Sailing Club, (RYA 1974/4, IYRU Case 69), refer.

The case of *Bald Eagle* v *Poseidon* is of added importance because it laid down that, when B1 has established an overlap between A1 and the shore or bank, in accordance with rule 42.3(f), B1 is entitled to room to pass a further obstruction consisting of a projection from the original obstruction, provided that her overlap is established before A1 is within two lengths of the second obstruction.

4. When B1 establishes such an overlap some distance from the shore, A1, now L2, may luff head to wind if she pleases to prevent B1, now W2, from passing, and if L2 succeeds in breaking the overlap and reaches the shore clear ahead, then (1) above applies.

5. When, as in Fig. 61 L2 luffs and W2 maintains her overlap until the shore is reached at L3 W3, then rules 38.5 (Curtailing a Luff) and 42.1(a) (Room at Marks and Obstructions when Overlapped) and the cases of *Lil* v *Verena* (YRA 1886), *Mimosa* v *Preciosa*, (YRA 1905/7), *Patience* v *Sea Thrift* (RYA 1957/6) and the Hunts Sailing Club (RYA 1974/4; IYRU Case 69) refer: W3 is entitled to room, and L3 cannot luff W3 ashore or into any kind of danger.

6. When the yacht clear ahead, A2 in Fig. 61, is not sailing as close to the lee shore as she could, and at that time there is room for B2 to establish an overlap to leeward of A2 and to pass between A2 and the lee shore, then, as in (5) above, A2, now W the outside yacht, must give B2, now L the inside yacht, room to pass between W and the shore. If, however, A2 reaches the shore clear ahead of B2, then (2) above applies. Rules 37.1, 38.5 (Curtailing a Luff) and 42.1(a), and the case of *Astrild* v *Eelin* (YRA 1900/2) refer.

7. In (2) above, the case of *Myth* v *Rampant*, (RYA 1953/6) set the precedent that A2, in Fig. 60, having denied B2 a leeward passage, is entitled to luff B2 when she has no alternative but to try to pass to windward of A2. Furthermore, having luffed B2 out into the stronger foul current, A2 can bear away again for the slack water in-

shore provided that, when B2 follows her and protests under rule 39 (Same Tack—Sailing below a Proper Course after Starting), A2 can satisfy the protest committee that in so doing she did not sail below a proper course. Should B2 drop clear astern of A2 and then establish an overlap to leeward before A2 again reaches the shore, (6) above would apply.

8. When there is a considerable gap in the shore line, such as a river mouth or bay, across which the yachts must sail before again reaching the general shore line again, the case of *Devil of Staines* v *Cascade* (RYA 1959/14) set the precedent that, when there is sufficient room and distance for B1 or B2 in Fig. 61 to establish an inside overlap on A1 or A2 before either reaches the far side of the gap, B1 or B2 can do so. Hence, if the yacht clear ahead wants to preserve the *status quo*, she must sail into the gap to prevent the yacht clear astern from establishing an inside overlap.

9. In all cases where a yacht clear astern tries to establish an inside overlap on the yacht clear ahead and pass between her and the shore, the onus is on the yacht clear astern to satisfy the protest committee that the overlap was established in proper time in accordance with rule 42.3(d), and that there was room for her to pass between the yacht clear ahead and the shore.

10. When A1 or A2 in Fig. 60 is sailing as close to the shore as she deems prudent, although rule 34 (Hailing) is not mandatory, it is a seamanlike practice for her to hail B1 or B2: 'I'm alongside the shore, don't try to come inside me,' or words to that effect. This will, on the one hand, caution B1 or B2 that there is no water between A1 or A2 and the shore and, if after that warning B1 or B2 persists in forcing a passage and either touches A1 or A2 or runs aground, she does so at her own peril; on the other hand, such a hail would strengthen A1's or A2's case in any protest.

11. Although the onus lies on the yacht clear astern in accordance with rule 42.3(d), it is important that the rights of the yacht clear ahead should be protected only when she is actually sailing as close to the shore as, in the circumstances, a reasonable and experienced helmsman would deem prudent. If it becomes understood that A1 in Fig. 60 sailing over a foul current somewhere near the shore cannot be passed to windward, things become altogether too easy for her—if she keeps just on the edge of the current, it is practically impossible for B1 to pass to leeward of her either. These remarks equally apply when A2 is sailing over a foul current somewhere near the lee shore, and B2 tries to pass to windward.

12. In the case of the Bristol Avon Sailing Club (RYA 1978/5) see Fig. 62. P was sailing up river close-hauled on port tack very close to the bank. S was unable to point as high and had been forced away from the bank, tacked to starboard and hailed 'Starboard!' to P. P counter-hailed for room, being unable to keep clear of S without either luffing into the bank or bearing away, when the current would have carried her on to S. There was no collision and neither yacht protested. The race officer saw this incident and was concerned because he could not find a rule in Part IV to cover it and asked for advice. The answer was that S, having tacked onto starboard, could establish rights under rule 36 (Opposite Tacks—Basic Rule) only provided that she first complied with rule 41.2 (Tacking or Gybing), by tacking far enough from P to enable her to keep clear, without having to begin to alter her course until after S's tack was completed. If, on the one hand, S discharged the onus of satisfying the race committee that she completed her tack in time, then P infringed rule 36 by holding her course. It seems from the diagram that, had P kept a proper look out and had exercised intelligent anticipation, as soon as S completed her tack to starboard P should either have eased sheets and slowed down to allow S to cross ahead of her and tack, or borne away

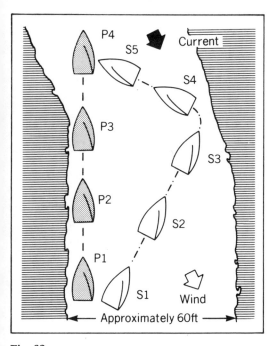

P4
S5
Current
S4
P3
S3
P2
S2
P1
S1
Wind
← Approximately 60ft →

**Fig. 62**

immediately and passed astern of S. The case of *Tartar* v *Sprite* (YRA 1913/2) refers.

If, on the other hand, S completed her tack in a position from which it was impossible for P to keep clear, the onus placed on S by rule 41.3 would make it extremely difficult for her to satisfy the protest committee that she complied with rule 41.2.

It is not open to P to hail for room, since this hail is governed by rule 43 (Close-Hauled, Hailing for Room to Tack at Obstructions), which applies only to close-hauled yachts on the same tack approaching an obstruction.

13. Having dealt with fixed obstructions such as the shore, shoals, banks, etc, it is important to remember that rule 42.3(f) also applies to a moving obstruction consisting of 'another vessel', and the cases of St. Mawes Sailing Club (RYA 1966/6; IYRU Case 27) and *W* v *M* (USYRU Appeal No. 163, 1974; IYRU Case 67) refer. As these cases are brief and should be self-explanatory, they are given *verbatim*.

## IYRU Case 27 (St Mawes Sailing Club; RYA 1966/9)

The case concerns (1982) rule 42.3(f), when there are several overlapping yachts, each of which is just clear of the yacht on either side of her, other yachts clear astern, coming up with more wind must keep clear. When, after a reaching start, several yachts approach an obstruction together, how should the right of way between them be determined?

*Problems.* Position 1 in Fig. 63 shows the yachts soon after the start. All are heading for an obstruction on the course—a rocky headland about half-a-mile away which must be left to port. Position 2 shows the yachts three hundred yards or so from the headland.

A, who thought that B was clear astern at the start, does not want to luff as she is already afraid that she will be badly by the lee when she reaches the headland and will have to gybe if she is any more to windward.

1. As between A and B who has to keep clear if:
   (a) A was clear ahead at the start;
   (b) A was not clear ahead of B?

On the way to the headland, yachts A to K, each one of which has an overlap on the yachts on either side of her, run into a softer patch of wind and X, Y and Z come roaring up with a really vicious little squall and barge into the boats ahead as indicated at position 2. In every case there is room for X, Y and Z to poke their bows in the line without fouling anyone, but not room to sail through unless everyone pulls in his sheets.

2. Who makes room for X who makes her first overlap to leeward of the yacht ahead of her?
3. Who makes room for Y who makes her overlaps to windward and to leeward almost simultaneously?
4. Who makes room for Z who makes her first overlap to windward of the yacht ahead of her?

*Answers*
1. (a) If A was clear ahead of B, B, as the yacht clear astern under rule 37.2, must keep clear.

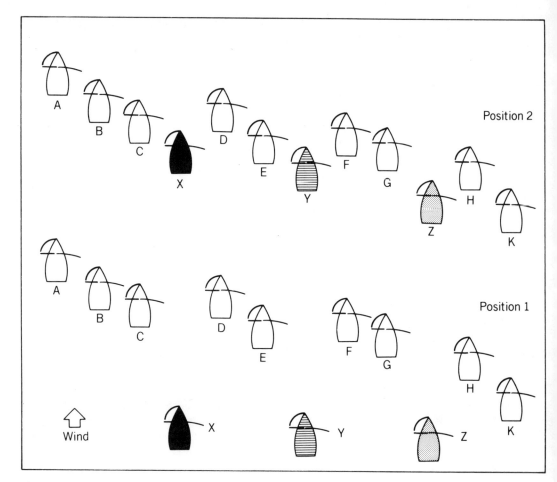

**Fig. 63**

(b) As soon as B establishes an overlap to leeward of A, A becomes bound by rule 37.1 and B by rule 37.3.

2, 3 and 4. As it is stated that there was not room for X, Y and Z to sail between the respective overlapping yachts, 'unless everyone pulls in his sheets', rule 42.3(f) applied. X, Y and Z were bound to keep clear because, at the time the overlaps were established, there was not room to pass in safety with regard to C and D, E and F, and G and H respectively.

If X fouled C, she would infringe rule 37.3. If X fouled D, she would infringe rule 37.1 and the same principle applies to Y and Z.

**IYRU Case 67 (W v M—USYRU Appeal No 163, 1974)**

The case concerns rules 42.3(a)(ii) and 42.3(f) governing restrictions on establishing an overlap, and establishing an overlap when passing a continuing obstruction.

*Facts and Conclusions*

When running on the last leg, W in Fig. 64 established an overlap on L not quite two lengths to windward of her, and subsequently M established overlaps on both yachts between them from clear astern. All three yachts finished without any narrowing of the space

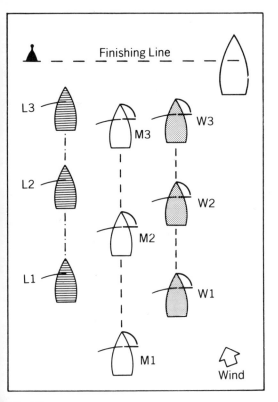

L3

L2

L1

Finishing Line

M3

W3

M2

W2

M1

W1

Wind

**Fig. 64**

between L and W and without contact, but W protested M for taking room to which she was not entitled under rule 42.3(a)(iii).

The protest committee disallowed the protest, holding that no infringement of rule 42.3(a)(ii) had occurred since L and W had left room for M to pass safely between them. W appealed.

*Decision of the appeals committee*
    Rule 42.3(a)(ii) says that:

> A yacht *clear astern* may establish an inside *overlap* and be entitled to room . . . only when the yacht *clear ahead* is outside two . . . lengths of the . . . obstruction except . . . as provided in rule 42.3(f).

L and W were within two lengths of each other. By definition, obstructions include craft under way if they are large enough, so that each of the three yachts, L, M and W, was an obstruction to the other two. W had estab-

lished her overlap on L from clear astern and was attempting to pass her. Inasmuch as this did not occur quickly or in a short distance, L was a continuing obstruction to W. Rule 42.3(f) states that:

> A yacht *clear astern* (in this case M) may establish an *overlap* between the yacht *clear ahead* (W) and a continuing *obstruction* (L) . . . only when at that time there is room for her to pass between them in safety.

In this case there was room for M to establish an overlap in safety between L and W. M's action is supported by rule 42.3(f). Accordingly, she infringed no rule and the appeal against her is dismissed.

## Hailing for Room to Tack

Excluding off-shore courses and those set in unobstructed waters for principal events, there must be few races in which at some stage two or more close-hauled yachts do not approach the shore or the bank of a river, lake or reservoir. If helmsmen are to compete with one another at close quarters safely and fairly, they must know how to interpret and apply the rules governing such situations, so let us see how they work.

First, look at Fig. 65(a) and Fig. 65(b) and imagine that these situations occur in open water, clear of all obstructions. In such circumstances A, the yacht clear ahead in Fig. 65(a), cannot tack and cross ahead of B, the yacht clear astern (behind), without infringing rule 41, (Changing Tacks—Tacking and Gybing), and the same applies to L, the leeward yacht in Fig. 65(b), with regard to W, the windward overlapping yacht. Only the situation shown in Fig. 65(b) will be discussed since the comments also apply to Fig. 65(a).

When safe pilotage requires L to make a substantial alteration of course to avoid running aground or into some other obstruction, rule 43 (Close-Hauled, Hailing for Room to Tack at Obstructions) is specifically framed to over-ride rule 41 by giving L the right to hail W for room to tack to escape peril.

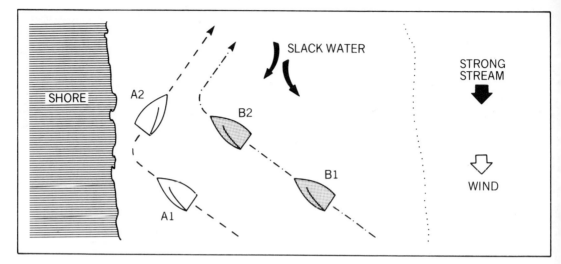

**Fig. 65a**

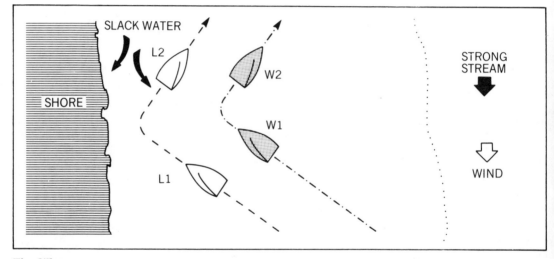

**Fig. 65b**

The first rule drafted by the Yacht Racing Association to govern this situation was 1876 rule 23 (Close hauled approaching shore) and read:

**23**  If two Yachts are standing towards a shore or shoal, or towards any buoy, boat, or vessel, and the Yacht to leeward is likely to run aground, or foul of such buoy, boat, or vessel, and is not able to tack without coming into collision with the Yacht to windward, the latter shall at once tack, on being hailed to do so by the owner of the leeward Yacht, or the person acting as his representative, who shall be bound to see that his own vessel tacks at the same time.

This rule has since been amended several times to make it more comprehensive and precise, but its principles have remained unchanged, a tribute to the 35 yachtsmen who drafted the YRA's first code of rules in 1876.

The four essential conditions that must be fulfilled before rule 43 can be invoked to over-ride rule 41 are:

1. Both L and W must be close-hauled on the same tack.
2. Both yachts must be approaching an obstruction.
3. Safe pilotage requires L to make a substan-

tial alteration of course to clear the obstruction.

## 4. L cannot tack without colliding with W.

Should there be a strong foul stream offshore and slack water inshore, rule 43 gives L a chance of gaining a considerable tactical advantage over W. When both yachts have tacked, as shown at L2W2, L2 becomes the windward yacht, and so placed can sail W2 out into the stronger stream as far as she likes. L2, however, can tack back towards the slack water—it may be possible to see where the slack water or eddy current ends—whereas W2 cannot hail or tack to escape her opponent's clutches because, although the foul stream doubtless is a considerable hindrance to W2, it does not rank as an obstruction. Hence, unless W2 eases sheets, loses way, drops astern of L2 and then tacks, she can only wait until L2 decides to tack and then follow suit. This restriction often causes W2 to lose several places.

This tactic is quite legitimate and fair, but for this reason it is all the more important that both yachts should strictly observe the rules in the following respects.

First when L reaches such a position that she believes she will run into danger by holding her course any farther—that is when safe pilotage requires her to make a substantial alteration of course to clear the obstruction— she must hail W loudly and clearly, so that her hail is capable of being heard by W. In the noise and commotion of wind and rough sea, it may sometimes be difficult to make W hear. The usual hail is 'Lee Oh!' or 'Water!'.

W must then accept L's hail as a warning that, of necessity, L must now tack to clear the obstruction. The fact that the obstruction may only be a soft, reed-fringed river bank and not rock-bound coast does not affect the application of the rule.

L must not approach the obstruction so closely before hailing that finally she is forced to hail and tack simultaneously. She must give W reasonable time and opportunity to respond and keep clear. Although it is well established that W is not required to take any anticipatory action before L hails, good seamanship demands that W must be on the alert for a hail and, when it is given, respond to it at the earliest possible moment. This is well documented, and the cases of *Red Jacket* v *Bluebell* (YRA 1938/6), *Greylag* v *Valhalla* (YRA 1947/7), *Susie* v *Wahoo* (RYA 1964/26) and *Pandora* v *Pax* (RYA 1969/8) refer.

On hearing L's hail, W must at the earliest possible moment allow L room to tack, but there is no compulsion on W to give room by tacking herself. No doubt in the majority of cases that is what she would normally do. So long as W fulfils that obligation, the rule does not specify how she is to carry it out. For example, W may either lose way by luffing until head to wind to let L cross ahead of her, or she may bear away and pass under L's stern into the slack water near the shore before tacking herself. In either case, in reply to L's hail, W must counter-hail, 'You tack' or words to that effect. Having so hailed the onus is on W to satisfy the race committee that she kept clear of L.

After hailing correctly, but before she begins to tack, L must wait until either she sees W luffing prior to tacking, or hears W's counter-hail. When W chooses the second alternative, it is obvious that she must notify L of such a decision by a prompt counter-hail. This is another reason why L is required to hail before she is in immediate danger of fouling the obstruction.

At the earliest possible moment after W responds to L's hail, L must begin to tack either before W completes her tack or, if L cannot then tack without touching W, immediately L is able to tack and clear her. L must not hail W and then, when W tacks, hold her own course closer to the obstruction before tacking herself. That is most unfair and a gross infringement of the rule.

The intention of rule 43 is that immediately W is hailed she must give L room to tack and L must tack immediately it is possible for her to do so.

So much for the rights and obligations of L and W under rule 43 when they are in the situation shown in Fig. 65(b). It is important to stress the fact that when L hails W for room to tack, W cannot refuse to respond except in Fig. 71 discussed below. Should W deem a hail unjustified, she should normally respond and then protest.

As long ago as 1880, the second edition of Dixon Kemp's *A Manual of Yacht and Boat Sailing* laid down the dictum that L is the sole judge of her own peril. That is because, at L1W1 in Fig. 65(b), L is closer to the obstruction, and W may be unable to see what is under L's lee bow or to judge whether it is necessary for L to tack. The obstruction may be semi-submerged rocks or posts, floating wreckage, or even a party of swimmers some distance off the shore, to mention but a few possibilities in what to W may appear to be open water. Its is a matter of good seamanship and common sense that W must respond to L's hail; W can argue about its necessity later at a protest hearing.

Reverting to the first two conditions essential to invoke rule 43, L has the right to hail W for room to tack only when both yachts are close-hauled on the same tack and are sailing towards an obstruction. Therefore, if L does not hail W while both are still on starboard tack and tacks to port, as shown in Fig. 66 at L2W2, so that she is sailing away from the obstruction when she meets W, close-hauled

on starboard tack, they are on opposite tacks and rule 43 does not apply; the situation is governed by the Opposite Tacks—Basic rule 36, under which L must keep clear, either by bearing away hard to pass under W's stern or by tacking back to starboard and then hailing W for room to tack. A double tack in such circumstances may cause L to lose steerage way and even go aground, but she must abide by the consequences of failing to hail before she tacked. She has no right to say to W 'I cannot tack for lack of water' and claim room to carry on. The ruling case on this point is that of *Bedouin* v *Halcyone*, (YRA 1885) and there have been many subsequent cases supporting that interpretation. L should have anticipated that the situation would arise and, had she hailed W before tacking, the onus would lie on W to give L room. Note that had L done this, rule 43.1 entitles L to room to tack and clear W. The case of *Electron II of Portsea* v *Combat* (RYA 1977/8) refers.

A common situation producing argument and potential danger occurs at Cowes when a number of yachts have started from the Royal Yacht Squadron's starting line on a beat to the westward over a foul stream (Fig. 67). Many yachts start close-hauled on starboard tack, heading inshore to cheat the stream, and when they are overlapping close abreast, L, on

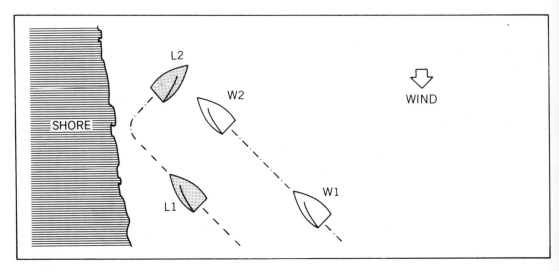

**Fig. 66**

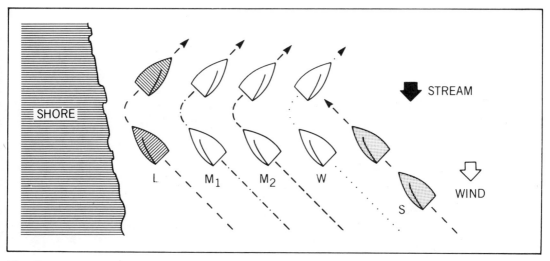

**Fig. 67**

approaching the rocks off the Green, hails M1 for room to tack. Before M1 can respond, she in turn must hail M2 and M2 must hail W, and only when W responds does it become a case of 'when Father turns we all turn'. The diagram shows five yachts in line abreast, but there may be a dozen or more, so for L's hail to pass from yacht to yacht right through the line necessarily takes time, and L must start hailing well before she is in actual danger of going aground.

This situation can become even more perilous when another close-hauled starboard-tack yacht, S, approaches the line of tacking yachts or yachts that have only just tacked to port, loudly hailing 'Starboard!' to W. If W now hails M2 'Water for S' and M2 passes this hail back through the line of yachts, there will almost certainly be chaos, collisions and L may be forced to go aground, completely nullifying the object of rule 43.1. As has already been explained, in such circumstances W should anticipate what inevitably will happen and, while she is still on starboard tack, hail S for room to tack. S must then give W room not only to tack, but also to clear S, and if S deems W's hail unjustified, S can protest. In any event, S would be wise to observe the precept of doing unto others as she would that they should do unto her, and avoid getting involved

in a shambles; in tomorrow's race she may easily find herself in W's position!

Such a predicament is by no means peculiar to Cowes; it frequently occurs in river racing when yachts are beating, but so long as all the yachts act in accordance with the rules—bearing in mind that they are specifically framed to enable yachts to compete with one another at close quarters in safety—they should be able to keep out of trouble and relish the excitement.

In this connection, it may be as well to stress the fact that the rules apply to all yachts, large and small, in all circumstances. Even though small dinghies, racing on a tideless water in a light breeze, may be able to bump into one another with no more damage than some loss of paint, or at worst a split plank, there is no excuse for failing to observe the rules. Some of their helmsmen may later steer large heavy-displacement yachts in rough seas, strong tidal streams and winds, along rock-bound shores, when a collision may result in a yacht being disabled or sunk or her crew being injured or killed. All helmsmen should therefore learn to observe the rules.

So far, situations have been discussed in which the obstruction is a stationary object, but the definition of an obstruction includes 'a vessel under way'. Up to 1960, the definition

**Plate 22**    Darings 5 and 1 short tacking off the Green at Cowes must give way to all yachts coming in on starboard tack, regardless of whether or not they are in the same race. The Darings cannot call for water, because they are in an opposite-tacks situation, so they must make up their minds in plenty of time whether they can cross ahead, or will have to bear away under the in-coming cruiser's stern (and probably under the rest of the fleet coming in behind her!)

read, 'craft under way (including another yacht holding right of way)', but in 1961 that phrase was amended to the present wording because its scope was too limited. Any vessel, racing or cruising 'on her lawful occasions' can rank as an obstruction under rule 43.1, whether or not she holds right of way under either IYRU racing rule 36 or the International Regulations for Preventing Collisions at Sea, Part D—Steering and Sailing rule 17(a)(i). For example, in a simple opposite-tacks situation where P unsuccessfully attempts to cross ahead of S, S cannot 'sail on regardless' and hit P causing serious damage. S is bound by good seamanship and either IYRU racing rule 32 (Avoiding Collisions), 'to make a reasonable attempt to avoid a collision', or IRPCAS rule 21, 'to take such action as will best aid to avert collision.' Hence, a give-way yacht that fails to keep clear also ranks as an obstruction.

Let us now study the application of the rules to the situation shown in Fig. 68, where PL and PW, close-hauled on port tack, are approaching S, close-hauled on starboard tack—incidentally, S need not be close-hauled to hold right of way under rule 36.

As between PL and PW, the Same Tack—Basic rule 37.1 applies, under which the leeward yacht, PL, holds right of way. As between PL and S and between PW and S, rule 36 applies and S ranks as an obstruction to both yachts. It will be seen that PL fulfils all four of the conditions essential to invoke rule 43.1, and therefore she has the right to hail PW for room to tack and PW must respond, even though PL has the alternative means of escape by bearing away to pass under S's stern. Situations like this often occur in open water, when PW may be quite unaware of S's proximity because she is hidden by PL's sails. In the

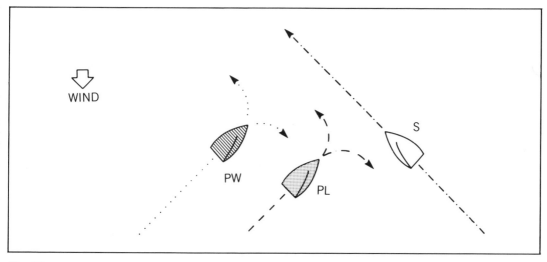

**Fig. 68**

interests of safety, it is vital that PL hails PW loudly and clearly and makes her understand why she is being hailed.

The ruling case on this point of law was that of *Sheldrake* v *Puffin; Teal* v *Sheldrake* (YRA 1934/1); a more recent case is that of the Laleham Sailing Club (RYA 1974/6).

On the other hand, should PL adopt the alternative means of keeping clear by bearing away and passing under S's stern, rule 42.1(a) (Rounding or Passing Marks and Obstructions) applies. This requires PL, as the outside yacht, to give PW, the yacht overlapping her on the inside, room to pass the obstruction on the same side if she wishes to do so. The following cases are relevant:

*Seahawk* v *Fundi* (RYA 1962/37; IYRU Case 6)

*Satan* v *Lilli* (RYA 1962/38)

*Lucky Dip* v *Crusoe; Crusoe* v *Lucky Dip* (RYA 1963/24; IYRU Case 16),

*Fury* v *Endeavour* (RYA 1963/4; IYRU Case 13)

*Maja* v *Undine* (RYA 1964/8)

*Barfly* v *Nausicaa* (RYA 1973/5)

*Lindy* v *Symphony* (RYA 1974/5)

Spinnaker Club of Ringwood (RYA 1975/2)

*N2986* v *N2716* (RYA 1980/6).

Finally, just to drive the point home, in the situation shown in Fig. 69 PL cannot invoke

rule 43.1 because she is not required to make an alteration of course to keep clear of S and, when PW also wants to pass astern of S, PL must give her room to do so, even though PW has the alternative means of escape by tacking. The ruling case on this point of law was that of *Moana* v *Victory* (YRA 1928/14).

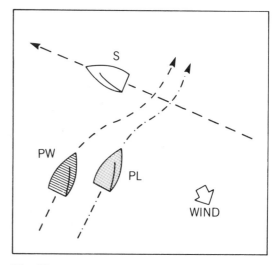

**Fig. 69**

The only limitation on L's right to hail W for room to tack is contained in rule 43.3 (Limitation on Right to Room to Tack, when the Obstruction is also a Mark). When, as shown in Fig. 70, W can fetch the windward mark and

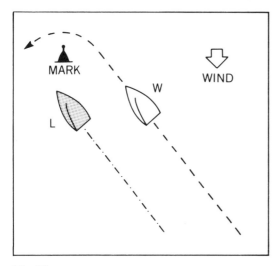

**Fig. 70**

L cannot, L has no right to hail. As the mark is surrounded by navigable water and the mark is not large enough to require L to make a substantial alteration of course to clear it, she is in no danger. She should exercise intelligent anticipation and either bear away to get room to tack, or gybe and make a 360° turn and then round the mark, or ease sheets, lose way, drop astern of W and tack. If L had the right to hail W, L would almost certainly round the mark ahead of W, which would be most unfair because W sailed the more weatherly course of the two and fully deserves to round the mark first.

But what happens when the obstruction or mark is large, such as a lightship, lightvessel or pier or, as shown in Fig. 71, a breakwater? In USYRU Appeal No 8, 1939, W and L were close-hauled on port tack approaching the finishing line near its leeward end. W could cross the finishing line and clear the breakwater while L could not. L, without hailing, tacked to starboard and hit W, who protested against her under rule 41.2 for tacking too close. The race committee disqualified L and she appealed.

The Appeals Committee ruled: 'L did not take advantage of the alternatives to sailing herself into an impossible situation such as: bearing away, or luffing, or easing her sheets

before reaching the breakwater so as to obtain room to tack without fouling W, and thereafter either establishing starboard-tack rights on W or passing astern of her. Since the breakwater constituted a mark which W could fetch, as well as an obstruction, L did not have the right to hail W about as provided in rules 43.1 and 43.2. In such a situation, rules 43.3(a) and 43.3(b) were applicable and W, after being hailed twice, would have been obligated to give L room to tack and clear the other yacht and L, upon receiving it, would have been required to retire immediately. The decision of the race committee disqualifying L is sustained.'

Lastly, when W in either Fig. 70 or Fig. 71 refuses to respond to L's hail and so informs L, but then fails to fetch the mark, W must either retire or accept an alternative penalty when so prescribed in the sailing instructions.

## A 'Hook' Finish

Appendix 12—Organisation of Principal Events, Section 7, paragraph (g)—Finishing line, specifies that the finishing line should be laid at right angles to the last leg of the course, and says it is desirable that yachts should pass through the finishing line at the end of each round so as to facilitate shortening the course when necessary. Although this appendix is designed to help race committees to provide the best possible conditions for principal events, these conditions should, whenever practicable, also be provided in ordinary club events.

Since the adoption in 1961 of one universally-approved code of racing rules, Part 1, Definitions, has ordained that:

A yacht *finishes* when any part of her hull . . . crosses the finishing line from the direction of the course from the last *mark* . . .

and it seems clear that a number of race committees do not understand what is meant by the 'last mark', and have not read the case law on this point. Some of their members have probably never looked at the definition.

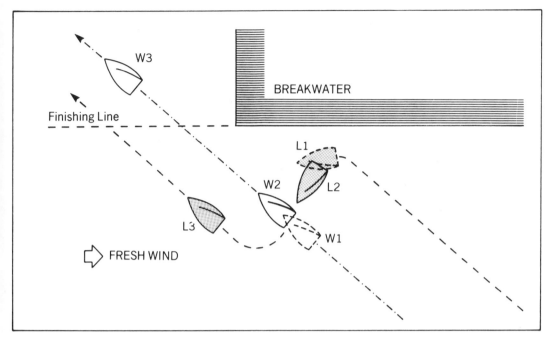

**Fig. 71**

**Plate 23**  Appeals have clarified the situation regarding finishing. The Laser will always be correct in finishing between the committee boat and the mark, assuming that the last mark is to the right of the photograph. If the sailing instructions say that she should round the outer distance mark to port before crossing the finishing line, these should be ignored because that is contrary to the definition of finishing, and her action would be upheld on appeal if not in the protest room.                                                                      *Fisher*

The following case law refers:

USYRU Appeal No. 84, May 29, 1961;
Whitstable Yacht Club (RYA 1963/26),
*Tam Pudden* v All other competitors (RYA 1975/1),
Army Sailing Association (RYA 1975/15),
*Faughan* v Race Committee (RYA 1979/1; IYRU Case 102).

A recent case is that of *Wings, Catapult, Jaborwok* and *Self Tapper* v *Wisp Osara, Bandersnatch* and *Sioux* (RYA 1980/2). The course set was; A, D, A, B, C, D as shown in Fig. 72, rounding all marks to port; three rounds. The course was shortened while the leading yacht was between marks A and D, and the actual course sailed was: A, D, A, B, C, D, A, D, finish.

The protestors maintained that they had finished correctly in accordance with the finishing definition by crossing the finishing line from the direction of the course from the last mark, A, leaving mark D to starboard, whereas the protestees rounded mark D to port and crossed the finishing line from the wrong (opposite) direction. The protestors pointed out that IYRU rule 3.1 (The Sailing Instructions), says that the sailing instructions shall not alter Part 1—Definitions.

The race committee dismissed the protests, affirmed that the protestees had sailed the prescribed course and observed that this type of finish had been described as 'difficult' but that did not say that it was illegal.

The RYA upheld the resulting appeal for the reasons given by the appellants, saying that a hook finish is always illegal. It explained that when mark D becomes the outer finishing limit mark, it ceased to be a rounding mark to be rounded as prescribed in the sailing instructions, and the finishing definition required it to be passed to starboard. Hence, the 'last mark' referred to in the definition means the last rounding mark prior to crossing the finishing line which, in this instance was mark A.

The RYA pointed out in the case of *Polly* v Race Committee (RYA 1965/1) that, if the race committee required yachts to pass through the finishing line in the same direction at the end of each round, this requirement could be met by laying an additional mark, E, somewhere between mark C and the finishing line and prescribing that mark E should be rounded or passed to port before crossing the finishing line.

When a number of classes sail different courses but use a common finishing line, this requirement could be very important. However, there is a club that apparently ignores the finishing definition and rule 3.1(a) because it thinks that by so doing finishes are made more exciting!

In the case under discussion, it follows that only those yachts which crossed the finishing line from the direction of the course from the last mark, A, leaving mark D to starboard, actually finished. But any other yachts which rounded mark D to port before crossing the finishing line could also qualify as having finished, provided that they exonerated themselves in accordance with IYRU rule 51.4 (Sailing the Course), and then finished as required by the definition.

In the appeal of *Faughan* v Race Committee, the RYA observed: 'that the case of *Polly* v Race Committee was decided when the rules were newly introduced' and at that time it was considered reasonable to permit a degree of flexibility in adjusting points scores. Since then, a number of appeals have been decided on the basis of the rule as it now stands, and the IYRU has deleted the case of *Polly* v Race Committee so that it no longer ranks as a precedent.

'The Council rules that it is not open to a race committee to over-ride the definition of Finishing, and the race committee is directed to allow the finishing positions to stand, in the sequence in which they finished, of the yachts that finished correctly in accordance with the definition of Finishing. If the race committee is satisfied that the course ordered by its executive, the race officer, was such that other yachts were prejudiced so as to alter the result of the race, it is open to the race committee to award points to such yachts, but it would not be equitable for such yachts to rank higher

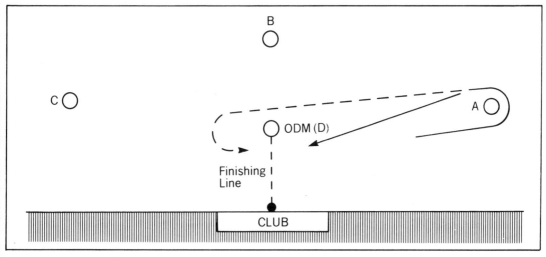

**Fig. 72**

than those that finished correctly.'

Although this last sentence is part of the RYA's ruling, it could be suggested that race officers and competitors alike should by this time be familiar with the intention of the rules and the definition. It should now be obvious that any race officer who sets a course that involves a hook finish is heading for trouble, and all competitors should ignore such an instruction, secure in the knowledge that the only legal way to finish is 'from the direction of the course from the last mark' and if they do so, they will be upheld on appeal.

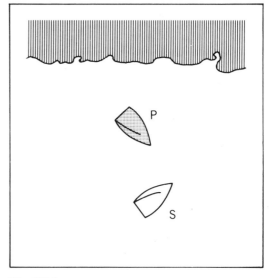

**Fig. Q7.1**

## Questions

**Q7.1** P has just tacked to clear a continuing obstruction in the shape of shallow water at the shore line. May she hail S for water, even though S is on starboard tack?

**Q7.2** May an outside leeward yacht with luffing rights luff an inside yacht not yet Mast Abeam, so that the latter has to pass the wrong side of a mark surrounded by navigable water? Or may the inside yacht call for water?

**Q7.3** Section C (Rules which Apply at Marks and Obstructions and other Exceptions to the Rules of Section B) over-rides those of Section B (principal Rights of Way Rules and their Limitations) except in certain cases. Which cases?

**Q7.4** When does a yacht finish?

# 8 Miscellany

## Anchoring and Weighing

Some while ago, a club secretary wrote to the Royal Yachting Association's Racing Rules Committee, saying that in his club there was a common belief that a yacht not manned but afloat at her preparatory signal was automatically disqualified, but no one could show him the actual rule that stipulated disqualification nor, after careful study of the rules book himself, could he find such a rule.

No yacht can be automatically disqualified without a hearing for infringing any rule, except as provided in rule 70.1—Action by Race or Protest Committee; that is to say only for failing to start or finish in accordance with the definitions, or for failing to report an infringement when certain other conditions are also fulfilled.

However, because there is a rule under which the yacht can be disqualified after a hearing, provided that she was moored and not anchored, it seems useful to examine the problem more closely. Indeed, such a rule has existed since the foundation in 1875 of the Yacht Racing Association. Its original rules were first published in 1876, and the New York Yacht Club has very kindly sent me photocopies of what is believed to be the sole surviving YRA rules booklet of that date—during World War II the YRA office in London was bombed and its contents destroyed.

One of these original rules read:

> *Anchoring.* 27. Yachts may anchor during a race, but must weigh their anchor again, and not slip. No yacht shall during a Race make fast to any buoy, stage, or pier, or send out an anchor in a boat, except for the purpose of Rule 24.

(Rule 24 of the 1876 booklet referred to running aground)

It is also necessary to explain the objects of this rule and to say why and when it was re-drafted, either to clarify its intent, or to relax some of its original severity.

These objects were, and are, to allow keel and centreboard craft to anchor at any time in light airs and foul tides, but to prevent them gaining an unfair advantage by late slipping of their moorings and, so far as centreboard craft are concerned, to prevent them launching from a slipway or hard close to the starting line just before the start.

Incidentally, the 1876 starting rule 17 provided for starts from anchors or moorings, lots being drawn for stations, with various restrictions regarding the use of springs and bridles, which if they were let go or parted before the signal to start, rendered the yacht liable to disqualification unless she could explain the reason to the satisfaction of the committee. This rule also provided for what was then known as a 'flying start', and up to 1899 it began:

> The yachts shall start from moorings, anchors, or under way, as directed by the Sailing Committee.

From 1900, starts from moorings were omitted and flying starts became the standard method.

The important point is that it is an essential part of the pre-starting manoeuvres, in order to start correctly in accordance with the rules, that (with certain exceptions) a yacht must be afloat and off her moorings or anchored during the period between her preparatory and starting signals.

**Plate 24**  Rights of way between yachts racing, some of which are legally anchored, will not be found in rule 63 – Casting Off, Anchoring, Making Fast and Hauling Out (that deals with the 'legally' bit); they will be found in rule 46 – Anchoring, Aground, Capsized or Person Overboard.

The anchoring rule has, over the years, been re-numbered, re-titled and re-drafted to meet changing requirements, and while some of the following cases are concerned with anchoring, they may also relate to means of propulsion because they involved the use of an anchor. Some cases, too, are rendered obsolete by subsequent rule amendments, but are described to explain these amendments.

In the case of *Katie* v *Hypatia* (YRA 1883), *Hypatia* was finishing in a calm, with the tidal stream running at an angle to the finishing line. She kedged close to the line and was then sheered across it; see Fig. 73. The committee, not knowing that *Hypatia* was anchored, fired a finishing gun for her.

On protest, she was disqualified, and on appeal the YRA ruled that not having weighed her kedge in accordance with the rule before

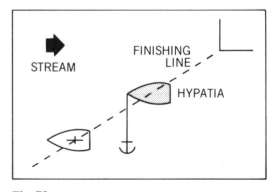

**Fig. 73**

crossing the finishing line, she had not therefore finished when the gun was fired. This is by no means a trivial or quibbling case, but one of considerable importance in calms and strong tideways.

In the *Minnow* case (YRA 1891), *Minnow* was disqualified because, during a calm, she was propelled by dropping her anchor and weighing it at her stem head at about ten-minute intervals. She claimed that she had the right to use to her own advantage any way or progress thus gained, and that it was un-doubtedly a common practice among racing yachts; the YRA upheld the committee's deci-sion. The somewhat similar case of the Royal Lymington Yacht Club (RYA 1979/5) de-scribed on p.107, occurred over 80 years later.

In the *Viera* case (YRA 1906/2) her crew were hauling the kedge up and felt it weigh but almost immediately catch on some obstruc-tion. As *Viera* gathered way in a sudden squall, the unexpected pull on the warp threw some of the crew down and the others let go to prevent themselves being dragged overboard.

*Viera* reported this loss in her declaration and maintained that, although the kedge was lost, it was weighed and not slipped, and that therefore she had not infringed the rule. She was disqualified and her appeal was dismissed.

When, in 1908, the International Yacht Racing Union published its first code of rules, YRA rule 27—'Anchoring during a Race' quoted above was renumbered but otherwise adopted almost *verbatim*.

In the *Britannia* case (YRA 1924/8), the yacht lost her kedge because the warp was frayed and cut, probably by some wreckage on the sea bed. She was disqualified because the kedge and warp were not recovered and car-ried on board during the remainder of the race, and because the rule as then worded admitted of no alternative.

The Royal Yacht Squadron submitted this case to the YRA as an instance of a yacht losing her kedge through no fault of her own, and suggested that perhaps some relaxation of the rule might be approved, to empower a committee to waive the penalty of disqualifica-tion in cases where entanglement in wreckage or unavoidable obstruction parted the kedge warp at the kedge.

The YRA replied that it recognised the hardship but, having regard to the consequ-ences that might occur, it could not recom-mend any amendment to the rule.

It should be noted in connection with these two cases that the 1982 rule 63.3, regarding the loss of an anchor, was first adopted as 1973 rule 63.1, and that it relaxes the severity of the earlier rule, without the feared consequences of doing so having materialised to date.

The Royal Sydney Yacht Squadron (YRA 1931/3) asked whether, after the preparatory signal had been made, a yacht hoisting her sails at her permanent moorings either in a position remote from, and out of sight of, the starting line or in the vicinity of the starting line infringed this rule. The YRA replied in the affirmative on both counts.

In the case of *Pelican* v *Polly*, YRA 1934/2, *Pelican* protested against *Polly* under this rule, because she was on her moorings at the prepa-ratory signal, *Polly* agreed that she was 'made fast' at the preparatory signal and cast off shortly afterwards. She argued that as the rule said: 'No yacht shall . . . *make* fast . . . and did not say: '. . . shall *be made* fast . . .' she did not infringe the rule.

The committee was of the opinion that it could not go beyond the strict wording of the rule and, since *Polly* did not make fast during the race, it dismissed the protest, but referred the case to the YRA which reversed the com-mittee's decision without comment.

As 1981 rule 63.2 (Casting Off, Anchoring, Making Fast and Hauling Out) allows a yacht to make fast by means other than anchoring '. . . to effect repairs, reef sails or bail out', it seems reasonable to suppose that a yacht can make fast to the shore, since she can be hauled out ashore, for the above purposes, but the point has not been tested.

In the *Lady Dainty* case (YRA 1939/7), when close-hauled on starboard tack she was struck by a port-tack yacht, breaking her port shroud. The port-tack yacht retired and helped *Lady Dainty* to make fast to the hard. It was then found that the only damage sustained was a sheared shackle-pin on the lower cross-tree. This was renewed and *Lady Dainty* cast off and continued in the race. She was disqualified for making fast, and her appeal was dismissed with the comment that the YRA recognised that the case was unfortunate for her. Here again, the current rule now permits such an action.

The case of *Susan Jane* v *Toucan*, (YRA1964/9) is unusual, in that the owners of these two Redwings and parties to the protest were both members of the YRA Council. One was chairman of the newly-appointed YRA Protest Committee—now the RRC—and the other was a member of it, as was the author. Their arguments were lengthy!

*Susan Jane* protested against *Toucan* for being on her moorings after the starting signal had been made. *Toucan* said that she had cast off her moorings before the preparatory signal, but the committee found that she was hand held alongside the quay while repairs and adjustments were being carried out, and disqualified her for being made fast. This decision was upheld on appeal.

There seems to be some slight uncertainty here. Clearly, according to rule 63.3, a yacht is 'anchored' when hand held by the crew standing on the bottom. But is she 'made fast by means other than anchoring . . . to effect repairs, etc.', when hand held by the crew standing on the shore?

In 1950, the words 'be hauled out' were added to make it clear that a centreboard craft hauled out ashore or on a pontoon was, for the purpose of this rule, 'made fast'.

When, in 1948, the rules were revised, the case of *Pelican* v *Polly* was taken into account and the rule was amended to include the words 'make fast'.

The Royal Northern Yacht Club (YRA 1950/11) asked whether a yacht whose kedge is on the course side of the starting line at the starting signal should be regarded as a premature starter (Fig. 74). The YRA replied in the affirmative, because the kedge is part of a yacht even when overboard.

The enormous increase in post-war centreboard classes produced some situations that had not previously occurred, mainly because most of the pre-war classes were keel boats. Here are two examples. First, a Cadet broke her jib halyard before the start. Her crew ran her ashore, pulled her over on to her beam

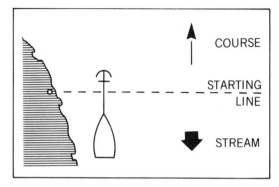

**Fig. 74**

ends, re-reeved the halyard, re-launched her and started in the race. Secondly, in heavy weather, a Sharpie was almost swamped, and her crew ran her ashore, bailed out, re-launched her and continued in the race. Both boats claimed that their actions were reasonable and sensible, but on protest and appeal they were disqualified because the rule did not permit such actions. The current rules treat them more realistically and allow them.

In the case of *Cromarty* v *Rockall*, (RYA 1954/16), owing to a strong foul current it was desirable to start in the slack water close under the windward bank. Two minutes before her preparatory signal, *Rockall* paddled out to this position, just short of the starting line, lowered her centreboard into the mud, thereby deliberately maintaining her position until the start, then raised her centreboard and sailed away. She was disqualified under the Means of Propulsion rule that prohibits checking way by abnormal means. The RYA ruled that such a procedure was contrary to that rule, adding that, in dismissing the appeal, it had borne in mind what is now the Fundamental Fair Sailing rule.

At this time, the Racing Rules Committees of the RYA and the NAYRU were working on drafting a universally-approved code of racing rules that came into force in 1961. The rules were chronologically grouped into six parts, according to who was responsible for observing them, the rule under discussion being put into Part V—Other Sailing Rules, Obligations of Helmsman and Crew in Handling a Yacht.

In a question from the Liverpool Sailing Club (RYA 1962/44;), it was stated that, on the one hand, it is contended that dinghies must sail over their anchors before they weigh them, or break what is now rule 60.1(d). On the other hand, the remainder feel that, so long as the anchor is not thrown forward when it is dropped, rule 63.3 makes it quite clear that it must be weighed before starting to sail again, it being quite immaterial that in so doing she acquires speed through the water.

The RYA answered that, provided the anchor is not thrown forward when dropped, the action of weighing it does not infringe rule 60.1.

The Itchenor Sailing Club (RYA 1963/29) asked the following questions relating to rule 60, Means of Propulsion, and rule 63, regarding the use of a centreboard to reduce speed, anchor or assist in manoeuvring a yacht before starting.

On Rule 63 it asked: '1. Does "a weight lowered to the bottom" imply the use of a line, as with a kedge-anchor?' To which the answer was yes. '2. Is it permissible for a centreboard housed in its normal box, to be lowered to the bottom to act as an anchor?' The RYA replied no. '3. Is a floatable centreboard, held down by shock-cord, considered to be a weight lowered to the bottom?' Again the reply was no.

On Rule 60 the questions were: '1. Does the *Cromarty* v *Rockall* decision (RYA 1954/16) still stand?' To which the RYA replied that, although the rules had been changed and the answer was no, the principle remains the same. '2. Is it permissible for way to be checked deliberately by lowering a centreboard, or a centreboard held down by shock-cord, into the ground?' The answer was no, although it was pointed out that the onus lies with the protestor to prove that the action was deliberate.

The club also asked whether it was permissible for a boat to check way at any time before the start by sailing close inshore into shallow water and deliberately lowering her centreboard into the ground, thus 'anchoring' on it in a preselected position near the windward end of a starting line? The same principle was held to apply as with the checking of way in the previous question and the answer was no.

The Stone Sailing Club (RYA 1963/30) asked some pertinent questions as to whether a yacht should be sailing at the preparatory signal. Saying that there appeared to be some divergence of opinion on this subject, it questioned whether there had been a RYA ruling or clarification that would resolve the question.

The queries that arose were: Should the yacht be sailing in the vicinity of the starting line at the preparatory signal with all crew on board? Or may she be afloat but not sailing and without the crew aboard? Or may the yacht be ashore or on a launching trolley?

The relevant rules that appear to show some ambiguity are: Rule 50 (Ranking as a Starter). This says that a yacht which sails about in the vicinity of the starting line between the preparatory and starting signals qualifies as a starter.

Rule 56 (Boarding). This rule does not allow any member of the crew to board the yacht after the preparatory signal (once the yacht starts racing). This would preclude a crew member from holding the yacht while launching after the preparatory signal, despite the allowance of rule 57 below.

Rule 57. (Leaving, Crew Overboard). This rule allows a crew member to leave a yacht and hold her anchored during a race, in the same way that a crew member would hold a yacht before launching.

Rule 59 (Outside Assistance). This rule implies that when the yacht is on a launching trolley at the preparatory signal, the trolley could be classed as 'gear other than that on board' being used.

In answer to the queries raised, the RYA said that a yacht must be launched and afloat, off her moorings or anchored at the preparatory signal. Also that rule 63.2 allows the crew to stand on the bottom and hold the yacht as a means of anchoring. Rule 63.2 permits a yacht to be run ashore or hauled out to effect repairs, reef sails or bail out. Rule 57 requires that a crew member who has left the yacht for any of the reasons given, must be back on board before the yacht continues in the race; rules 63 and 57 over-ride rule 56 in the above circumstances. (The cases of the Wellington Yacht and Motor Boat Association, New Zealand (RYA 1962/45) and the Bexhill Sailing Club (RYA 1962/46) refer.)

1981 rule 63.3 relaxed the requirement to recover an anchor to the extent that when, after making every effort, a yacht cannot recover an anchor or weight, she must report the circumstances to the race committee, which may disqualify her if it considers the loss due either to inadequate gear or insufficient effort to recover it. Rule 63.1 explicitly states that a yacht must be afloat and off moorings before her preparatory signal.

In the case of the Royal Lymington Yacht Club (RYA 1979/5; IYRU Case 105), *Anitra* kedged in a very light wind and foul tidal stream, just on the pre-start side of the starting line, and dropped back with the stream on a long scope of warp. At the starting signal she recovered her kedge, causing her to gather considerable way, cleared the starting line, crabbed across it a distance of some 50 yards and kedged again. She repeated this manoeuvre twice more, until she reached the slack water near the shore (Fig. 75).

*Anitra* maintained that she did not infringe rule 60 and, in support of her claim, cited the ruling (see p. 106) in the Liverpool Sailing Club (RYA 1962/44). Owing to a technicality, a protest against her was refused, so the race committee sought guidance from the RYA on this particular point, and asked the following questions: 1. Does the decision in RYA 1962/44 mean that the crew is entitled to haul up a kedge from a long way back, at any speed up to the maximum that is physically possible, and use the momentum thus gained to progress up tide or cross tide to a position that could not have been reached if the kedge warp had been hauled in slowly? 2. If the answer to question 1 is 'No', is there any other appeal decision or rule that limits the speed at which a kedge warp may be hauled in? 3. If the answers to questions 1 and 2 are 'No', would not some existing ambiguity be removed by strengthening either rule 60 or rule 63, to make it clear that the rapid hauling of a kedge warp or chain, so as to give a yacht appreciable way over the ground at the point where the anchor is raised, infringes rule 60?

The RYA then replied that the decision did

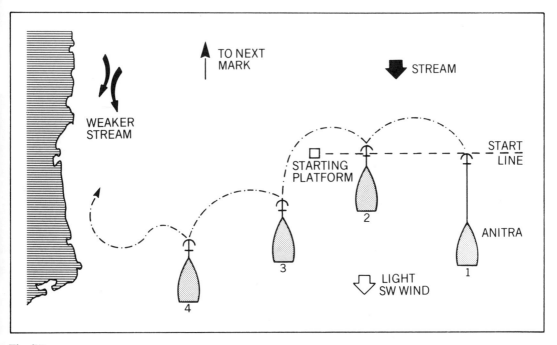

**Fig. 75**

not entitle a yacht to weigh her kedge in this way, although there was no appeal decision or rule specifically on this point. On the third question it observed that a yacht that recovers her anchor so quickly that she gathers considerable way over the ground at the point where the anchor is weighed or lifted off the ground, infringes rule 60 (Means of Propulsion), and that the RYA intended to submit to the IYRU an amendment to rule 60 to clarify this point

Although RYA 1962/44 and this case can be differentiated because, in the former, the kedge was hauled in once only, the IYRU RRC later decided to omit this from the Interpretations and to insert RYA 1979/5 as Case 103, because it is more comprehensive and explicit.

Finally, at its 1980 meeting, the IYRU RRC approved rule 60.1(d) for insertion in the rules.

# Man Overboard

The following incident occurred during the 1979 Weymouth Olympic Week in the International 470 class. K396 saw the helmsman of K491 in the water holding on to the side of an inflatable rescue boat about 50 ft from his own boat. K396 protested against K491 because she had finished the race after she had infringed rule 59 (Outside Assistance).

It was established that the helmsman of K491 fell out of the boat, which did not capsize, and the crew took charge of her. The helmsman wore a life jacket but could not swim. When the rescue boat approached, he held on to her until his crew sailed the boat back and came alongside the rescue boat. The helmsman then climbed into the rescue boat and from her into his own boat and continued in the race.

The decision of the protest committee was influenced by three points. First in the absence of the rescue boat, the helmsman might well have been in peril and a man overboard must always be regarded as being in peril to some extent; secondly, K491 was sailed back to her helmsman, so that she gained no advantage in distance; and thirdly the United States Yacht

Racing Union Appeal No. 161, 1974, IYRU Case 66, seemed to be completely relevant. In that case, shortly after gybing round the beam mark, the crew of *Polecat* fell overboard. Her helmsman took several minutes to lower the spinnaker and prepare the yacht to return to the crewman in the water, during which time the yacht made little or no forward progress. Meanwhile, a spectator boat picked up the crewman and offered to take him ashore. Instead, he was put back on board *Polecat* and she resumed the race. After finishing, *Polecat* elected to retire in view of rule 59. She subsequently sought reinstatement on the grounds that, in the interests of safety, the penalty of retirement points was too severe.

Both the Protest Committee and the US District Appeals Committee held that *Polecat* had received outside assistance and that her retirement under rule 59 had therefore been appropriate, but each body in turn urged *Polecat* to appeal to her national authority against the decision, which she did.

The USYRU Appeals Committee ruled: 'While rule 59 generally precludes a yacht from receiving outside assistance, it also contains a specific exception in the circumstances of rule 58, (Rendering Assistance), where the assistance is rendered to a vessel or person in peril. In the best interests of safety, a man overboard normally should be considered to involve some degree of peril; no countervailing circumstances appear here. Further, *Polecat* met the requirements of rule 57, (Leaving, Crew Overboard), namely, the man overboard was back on board before she continued in the race, for the protest committee found that *Polecat* made "little or no forward progress" during the recovery operation. Accordingly, *Polecat's* appeal is sustained and she is reinstated in her finishing place.'

The WOW protest committee decided to follow this IYRU interpretation, dismissed K396's protest and reinstated K491 in her finishing place. Incidentally, it may be of interest to record that the protestor had been a member of the RYA RRC until he had recently resigned and both he and the protestee seemed quite happy with this decision.

## Innocent Victims

There are some experienced members of protest committees who are unwilling to exonerate a yacht that has been forced by the illegal action of a second yacht to infringe a rule with regard to a third yacht, so a discussion of the official rulings in such situations may be helpful.

The principle that a yacht should be regarded as an innocent victim of another's infringement of the rules is well established, and rule 74.4 (Penalties) now reads in part:

> in consequence of her neglect of any of these **rules**, a yacht has compelled other yachts to infringe any of the **rules** she shall be disqualified . . . and the other yachts shall be exonerated.

The original decision of an American case, USYRU Appeal No. 11, 1940, did not support this principle, and it is discussed because it shows how the attitude towards the principle has subsequently changed when applied to the fairly common situation shown in Fig. 76.

It must be realised that, although the proximity of the mark obviously influenced the yachts' manoeuvres, it can be ignored so far as the application of the rules governing the situation is concerned. The situation must be examined as though it occurred in open water.

Another point is that protest committees should bear in mind the fact that when dealing with a situation involving three or more yachts and perhaps two or more protests, in order to decide correctly which yacht(s) is at fault it is essential to hear the evidence of all the yachts involved in the incident together. For example, when S in Fig. 76 protests against PL and PL protests against PW, and the protest committee hears the protests separately, it can easily misdirect itself. Assuming that the protest S v. PL is heard first, PL's defence may well be that PW prevented her from keeping clear of S, so PW must be present to hear PL's allegation and be given the chance of refuting it. If the protest S v. PL has already been started, as soon as PL makes her allegation the hearing should be adjourned until PW attends, and then re-opened.

The facts and decision of Appeal No. 11 given below are those in the original case. PL and PW were approaching a port-hand mark, both close-hauled on port tack, PW half a

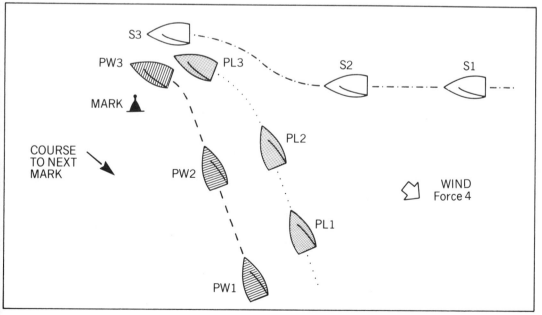

**Fig. 76**

length to windward and half a length astern of PL. PW hailed PL for room at the mark, PL seeing S approaching them close-hauled on starboard tack and realising that a collision might occur if they held their respective courses, hailed PW for room to tack, but PW did not respond. S was compelled to luff head to wind to avoid a collision. S protested against PL under the Opposite Tacks—Basic Rule 36, PL protested against PW under rule 43.2 (Close-Hauled, Hailing for Room to Tack at Obstructions). The race committee upheld both protests and disqualified PL and PW.

PL appealed and said she did not bear away to pass under S's stern because she thought that this would cause a collision. The race committee disagreed with this; it said that when four boat's lengths from the mark PL could quite safely have borne away, but as it was, both PL and PW held their port-tack courses and, in so doing, compelled S to luff to avoid a collision.

The NAYRU Appeals Committee decided that 'S being close-hauled on starboard tack had right of way over PL close-hauled on port tack under the Opposite Tacks—Basic Rule 36. We find nothing in the rules which deprived S of her right of way. (Two expert yachtsmen on board the committee boat had given evidence before the race committee that PL had room to bear away).

'If we accept the opinion of the two experts, PL had room to bear away and therefore was clearly at fault in not so doing. By accepting PL's contention that she did not have room to bear away without danger of collision with S, the question raised is whether, being in this predicament, she acquired right of way over S in spite of rule 36.

'We find that PL got herself into this predicament and must take the consequences. As PL and PW approached the mark and were in danger of collision with S, PL had a choice of whether to hail PW about or bear away under the stern of S. PL chose the former alternative, but PW failed to go about. The only course therefore left for PL, in order to avoid a collision with S, if possible, was to bear away under the latter's stern. PL took the risk that

PW might not tack. It cannot be assumed that all yachts in a race will obey the rules in every particular. PL ought to have hailed PW in time, so that if PW failed to tack, PL would have had the opportunity to bear away under the stern of S. Failure to hail in time to provide for possible contingencies was the fault of PL, which caused her later to foul S. The rules provide no excuse for such failure.

'S was within her rights throughout. It was S which, by luffing, avoided a collision with PL at the mark. PL, on the contrary, caused risk of collision by continuing on her course on the port tack, while S was on the starboard tack. S had done nothing to warrant her being deprived of her right of way, and the predicament into which PL sailed was through no fault of S and she ought not to suffer because of it. It is clear that if S did not have the right of way, it was because PL had it. But this would be directly contrary to rule 36 which in this respect at least is not qualified by any other rule. For these reasons we affirm the decision of the race committee.'

This decision represented the considered opinion of the NAYRU Appeals Committee forty years ago. It did not support the principle of regarding PL as the innocent victim of PW's failure to observe rule 43.2.

A very similar situation occurred in open water in the case of *Trojan* v *Grace Darling*, (YRA 1956/16); see Fig. 77. S, close-hauled on starboard tack, hailed PL, close-hauled on port tack. PL did not respond immediately, but eventually tried to tack too late. S tried to avoid PL but could not do so and a collision occurred, S hitting PL near her transom at PL2S2.

PL said she was on port tack with PW overlapping her to windward. When S hailed 'Starboard', PL hailed PW for room to tack. PW did not immediately respond, so PL hailed again. When PW did tack, then PL followed immediately, and very shortly after, the collision occurred. When S informed PL of her intention to protest, PL promptly protested against PW. PW shortly after capsized and retired, so PL withdrew her protest.

The protest committee found that initially

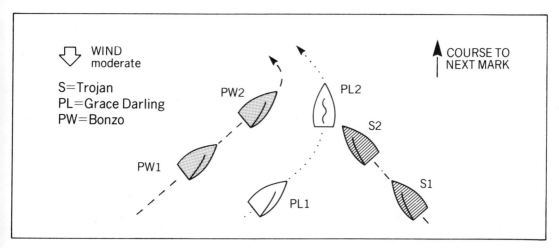

**Fig. 77**

PL had three options open to her: to cross ahead of S, to go astern of S or to hail PW for room to tack.

Before position 1 was reached, PL's intention had been to cross ahead of S but, realising she would be unable to do so, hailed PW for room to tack. When PW did not respond, PL still had time to go under S's stern. However, she hailed PW again, not knowing that PW might again ignore the hail, meanwhile sailing into a more and more awkward position with regard to S.

When S and PL were questioned as to positions, distances, speeds and times, their evidence was so similar that the protest committee decided not to take evidence from PW and, as she had retired, not to proceed against her. PL did not fully tack, she only luffed or may have passed through the wind when the collision occurred, so there was no question of her having infringed rule 41.

The protest committee remarked: 'It is realised that the racing rules do not order a port-tack boat to go astern of one on starboard, but they do insist that the port-tack boat shall keep clear. It was PL's duty to keep clear and this she did not do. By holding her course, PL had hoped to sail clear ahead of S, but in fact sailed into a position where she relied on PW to tack as well as PL, for PL to keep clear. If at the first hail, or shortly after, or even before,

PL had borne away, the incident would not have arisen.

'The protest committee upheld S's protest and disqualified PL, who appealed. The grounds were that she was prevented from tacking clear by PW, which did not respond at once to the hail, 'Water for a starboard boat', given in plenty of time. PL cited the cases of *Sheldrake* v *Puffin; Teal* v *Sheldrake* (YRA 1934/1) and *Little Jean* v *Farandole; Farandole* v *Little Jean* (RYA 1955/20). In the latter case the race committee found that P could have gone under S's stern, but the YRA did not find her under any obligation so to do, and had upheld her appeal.

PL pointed out that if her appeal failed, it would appear that in a similar situation a yacht in PL's situation was denied the right to hail a yacht represented by PW for room to tack, for fear that PW would not respond.

The RYA upheld PL's appeal and stated: 'From the findings of the committee it is evident that PL hailed PW in proper time and was entitled to expect room to tack. Nothing in the rules compelled PL to go under the stern of S or to anticipate PW's failure to comply with rule 43.2.

'In cases such as this, a boat in PL's position would be well advised to pursue her protest, even though the boat protested against retires. It is only because in this case there is no doubt

**Plate 25**    Team racing calls for a thorough understanding of the rules, and many a competition has been won or lost in the protest room.    *Nicypicy*

as to the facts that it is possible to uphold the appeal.'

Here then, in upholding PL's appeal, the RYA established the principle of the innocent victim, which directly conflicted with the NAYRU's decision.

Now for the sequel. Following the adoption of the 1961 IYRU racing rules, the NAYRU Appeals Committee updated and conformed its past appeals to the revised rules, and in 1969 modified its description of and its decision in Appeal No. 11 as follows: 'PW and PL (Fig. 76) were obligated under Rule 36 to keep clear of S while on the port tack, and under Rule 41.1 while tacking. PW hailed PL for room at the mark pursuant to Rule 42.1(a), which necessarily included room to pass astern of the obstruction S if PW elected to do so. PL hailed PW for room to tack to clear the obstruction S, but PW failed to respond either by

tacking or by giving PL room to tack as provided in Rule 43.2. PL was entitled to hail PW for room to tack and, had PW responded as she should have, both yachts would have tacked before reaching the mark, and PW would no longer have had an inside overlap or any claim for room. PW is disqualified for infringement of Rule 43 in failing to respond to a hail for room to tack. She also infringed Rule 41.1 for not keeping clear of S while tacking.

'When PW failed to respond to PL's hail for room to tack, PL was faced with the necessity of taking alternative action, if she could, to avoid fouling S. This raises the question of whether she should be exonerated as a victim of another yacht's foul as contemplated in Rule 72.1(b) (now rule 74.4—author). It is reasonable to assume that all yachts in a race know and will obey the rules, but discreet to anticipate that in some circumstances they may not.

PL claimed that she did not bear away under the stern of S because she thought that with the type of boat and the strength of the wind a collision would result. Two expert Scow skippers aboard the committee boat, however, gave their opinions that she could have borne away safely or slacked her sheets at four lengths from the mark. The decision of the race committee disqualifying PL for infringement of rule 36 is therefore sustained.'

Thus, when the NAYRU up-dated and conformed this appeal to the 1969 IYRU racing rules, it did not completely accept the principle of the innocent victim in this particular situation. However, it seems that it had already done so in Appeal No. 44, 1951, which stated in part: 'Since M (the intervening yacht) was the victim of another yacht's neglect of the rules, namely, L's improper luff, she was correctly exonerated from failing to keep clear of W-S.' And also in Appeal No. 95, 1964, which stated in part: 'The facts show that PW infringed Rules 42.2 and 37.1 and she was properly disqualified. She could also be disqualified under rule 72.1, in that she compelled PL to foul S and, accordingly, the appeal of PL is sustained and her disqualification is annulled.'

The following British cases also support the principle: *Orisha II* v *Neon Tetra* (RYA 1962/24) and *Maja* v *Undine* (RYA 1964/8; IYRU Case 18).

Hence, when a protest committee is satisfied, from the facts found at the hearing of two or more protests together arising from what is really one incident, that one yacht was compelled by the illegal action of a second yacht to infringe the rules with regard to a third yacht of which she was required to keep clear, the first yacht can be regarded as an innocent victim and exonerated.

## Means of Propulsion

Certain infringements of rule 60, (Means of Propulsion), were described under the heading Anchoring and Weighing (see page 102), and here are some others that have occurred under various provisions of this rule.

## Rowing

When formulating its original code of rules, the Yacht Racing Association's first rule relating to this subject was:

> *Sweeps.* 26. No towing, sweeping, poling or pushing, or any mode of propulsion except sails, shall be allowed.

In those days yacht racing was confined to heavy-displacement keel boats, and Dixon Kemp's *Manual of Yacht and Boat Sailing*, Dictionary of General Information, second edition, 1880, states: 'To sweep is to impel by sweeps, or large oars; formerly, vessels as large as 300 tons used sweeps, and by hard work could make three knots . . . '.In 1879, the YRA ruled that an oar could not be used to assist a yacht going from one tack to another.

In the *Petrel* case (YRA 1927/9) and in that of the West Cheshire Sailing Club (RYA 1954/33), the council ruled that nothing in the spirit or letter of the rules allows a boat to row during a race, even to escape peril, and if she does so, she must accept the consequences.

## Sculling

The practice of sculling a small boat by 'tiller waggling' is quite an effective means of propulsion, and is prohibited. However, in light airs it is very helpful to scull in this way when a yacht has little or no steerage way and will not come about. In the case of the Eastern Yacht Club (YRA 1889), it was ruled that to scull with a tiller to alter a vessel's course could not be considered an infringement of the rule. This interpretation was supported in USYRU Appeal No 56, 1954, which ruled that the helmsman of *Eastwind*, in almost calm conditions, moving his tiller to starboard several times before rounding a mark and several times to port after rounding it, did not bring the tiller beyond amidships, the purpose and result of his actions being only to alter the course of his yacht. Because he did not give her headway, his actions did not constitute an infringement of rule 60.

Before proceeding further, in order to understand the reasons for the decisions of the cases that follow, it is necessary to quote the current rule 60 (Means of Propulsion). This has been much revised and includes much of 1977 Appendix 2—'Pumping' sails, 'Ooching' and 'Rocking'.

## 60    Means of Propulsion

60.1    BASIC RULE

(a) Unless otherwise permitted by this rule, a yacht shall be propelled only by the natural action of the wind on the sails and spars, and the water on the hull and underwater surfaces. A yacht shall not check way by abnormal means.

(b) Sails may be adjusted and a competitor may move his body in order to change the angle of heel or fore and aft trim, or to facilitate steering. However, except as provided in rules 60.1(c) and 60.3, no actions, including *tacking* and *gybing*, shall be performed which propel the yacht faster than if the sails, hull and underwater surfaces had been trimmed to best advantage at the time.

(c) A yacht may promote or check way by means other than those permitted by this rule for the purpose of rule 58 (Rendering Assistance).

(d) A yacht may anchor as permitted by rules 63 (Casting Off, Anchoring, Making Fast and Hauling Out) and 64 (Aground or Foul of an Obstruction). A yacht shall not recover an anchor in a manner that causes her to pass the point at which the anchor is lifted off the ground.

60.2    ACTIONS THAT ARE PROHIBITED
Examples of actions which are prohibited except as permitted under rules 60.1(b) or 60.3:

(a) Repeated forceful movement of the helm (sculling).

(b) Persistent or rapidly-repeated trim-

ming and releasing of any sail (pumping).

(c) Sudden movement of the body forward or aft (ooching).

(d) Persistent or rapidly-repeated vertical or athwartships body movement.

(e) Movement of the body or adjustment of the sails or centreboard which leads to persistent rolling of the yacht (rocking).

60.3    ACTIONS THAT ARE PERMITTED
The following actions are permitted for the sole purpose of accelerating a yacht down the face of a wave (surfing), or when planing conditions exist, responding to an increase in the velocity of the wind.

(i) No more than three rapidly-repeated trims and releases of any sail (pumping).

(ii) Sudden movement of the body forward or aft (ooching).

There shall be no further pumping or ooching with respect to that wave or increase in wind.

In USYRU Appeal No. 91, 1962, two 8 ft cat-rigged El Toro dinghies, No. 842 and No. 2468, were reaching at almost hull speed in a 10 knot breeze, when the helmsman of No. 2468 made substantial movements of his tiller and consequent alterations of course, timed to the passage under his hull of each of several waves from the wash of a fast overtaking power cruiser. No. 842 protested against No. 2468 for an alleged infringement of rule 60.1. The race committee upheld the protest and disqualified No. 2468 which then appealed.

The appeals committee cited its Appeal No. 56, pointing out that in that case there was almost no wind and the helmsman was trying to alter the course of his yacht to round a mark. In the case of No. 2468, she was reaching at about hull speed in a 10 knot breeze, and sculling would have slowed her down and not increased her speed.

The statement in rule 60.1 that

> a yacht shall be propelled only by the natural action of the water on the hull . . .

recognises that taking advantage of wave action is a well-accepted part of yacht racing. The helmsman of No. 2468 made no rhythmical movements with the tiller in the absence of the power-boat waves. When a yacht is sailing at about hull speed, sculling is impossible, and in taking advantage of waves, a helmsman may move his tiller as he thinks best to accomplish that purpose. No. 2468's appeal was upheld.

## Rocking

The first appeal on this point of law was that of Stokes Bay Sailing Club v. *Allegro* (RYA 1957/16)—well before Appendix 2 was added to the rules in 1969—in which the crew of an Albacore dinghy admitted that he had continuously rocked for about an hour, but in his opinion this action did not infringe what was then rule 24, Means of Propulsion, which read in part: 'No yacht shall employ any means of propulsion other than the natural action of the wind on the sails.'

The race committee believed that the rule had been infringed because the action of the wind on the sails had been caused by the rocking, and the boat was not propelled by the natural action of the wind on the sails, as required by the rule. *Allegro* was therefore disqualified, but the race committee referred its decision to the RYA, which upheld it.

A similar case was that of *Drambuie* v. *Dandy Grad* (RYA 1962/42), in which the race committee found that *Dandy Grad* was deliberately and regularly rocked from side to side over a considerable part of the course. Although the race committee considered that this method of propulsion infringed the spirit of rule 60, it had been informed that it was fairly widely practised in certain classes and it therefore sought the decision of the RYA on its legality. *Dandy Grad* had refused to attend the hearing, telling *Drambuie* that her protest was frivolous and petty. The RYA ruled that to seek to propel a yacht by rocking infringes rule 60, and referred to the previous case.

Some very helpful guidance on this subject is found in USYRU Appeal No. 193, 1976, IYRU Case 82. The Austin Yacht Club requested an interpretation of rule 60 and an elaboration of old Appendix 2, for the purpose of establishing guidelines for onus of proof, evidence and facts pertaining to small dinghies in particular and all classes in general.

The club said that planing hull single-handed boats such as Lasers and Finns will persistently roll from side to side, or rock as defined in rule 60.2(e), owing to the natural action of wind and water while being sailed down wind. A helmsman can passively allow the rolling to persist, make efforts to stop the rolling, or initiate and/or promote the rolling with deliberate body actions which may or may not be easily discernible.

Alleged infringements of rule 60 by helmsmen of small boats are increasing, and are usually impossible to prove or disprove.

The USYRU Appeals Committee answered: 'While this request for interpretation is directed primarily to rocking, it makes reference to all of rule 60 and will be so treated.

'*Pumping* is clearly defined or described in rule 60.2(b) and the description need not be repeated here. Pumping is permitted when planing or surfing conditions exist, in order to promote planing or surfing. The test is whether or not the conditions are such that by no more than three rapidly-repeated trimming and releasing of any sail could a boat start surfing or planing. Planing is easy to recognise. A planing boat literally shoots forward over the water. When planing conditions exist, some boats will be planing some of the time.

'*Surfing* is just as simple to decide, though not so obvious. When a boat is riding a wave—i.e. surfing—she will rapidly gain a length or so on nearby boats which are not riding waves at the time. Subsequently, one or more of the other boats will be lifted by a wave for a short ride. This can best be observed from a position at right angles to a leg on which a line of boats is sailing.

'Judges and race committees should make it a point to observe and preferably record whether or not planing or surfing conditions exist, and

**Plate 26**   Keelboats such as this International Star can plane and surf. A jury must decide whether the conditions make it possible and, if so, whether any rapid sheet trimming is done only to promote such planing or surfing.                                                                                                     *Guy Gurney*

if the conditions change during the race, at what time planing or surfing conditions begin or cease as the case may be.

'*Ooching*, which consists of lunging forward and stopping abruptly, falls in the same category as pumping. This means that ooching is permissible only to promote planing or surfing, and only when planing or surfing conditions exist.

'*Rocking* consists of persistently rolling a yacht from side to side—which, needless to say, means being rolled by the crew. No mention is made of planing or surfing or of being in the same category as pumping. Accordingly, rocking is prohibited at all times. Obvious crew motion which induces persistent rolling is readily recognized as rocking. Recognition of more subtle rocking can be assisted by observation of the conditions and of the comparative performance of the yachts in the race. When waves are small or essentially non-existent, persistent, crew-induced rolling from side to side should be readily recognised by comparison with other boats whether or not crew motion is obvious, because most masts will be moving from side to side little if at all. When a sea is running, and particularly on a broad reach (but not limited thereto), masts will noticeably be swinging from side to side as the boats are rolled by passing waves. The motion is accentuated by the fact that some masts will be moving to port while others are moving to starboard. When the boat is not being rocked or the rolling is being reduced by crew counter motion, the rhythm will be imposed by the wave pattern. Any boat whose rhythm is different from and particularly whose rolling is more accentuated than the others may be guilty of being rocked.

'As to onus of proof, it is the responsibility of the protest committee to determine as best it can what happened, and only when testimony

**Plate 27** The lighter the boat in relation to her crew weight, the more effective rocking and other infringements of rule 60 (Means of Propulsion) become. Competitors and race committees should watch for tell-tale masthead movements. *Tim Hore*

is so conflicting or scanty that a judgement cannot be made, should the protest committee fall back on an onus provision as the basis for its decision, because the protest committee should know from its own observation whether or not planing or surfing conditions existed.

'When one competitor protests another for pumping or rocking, it is customary (but not obligatory), when the protestee denies the charge, to require the protestor to produce a witness as a protection to the protestee on a protest in which there is no possibility of the protestor being penalised. Usually there will be one or more witnesses to the alleged infringement, and they should be found and asked to testify by the protest committee, if not by the protestor. The performance of the protested boat with relation to two or more nearby boats may also support the alleged infringement.

'Competitors at the most experienced level

have indicated that pumping and rocking a boat around the course in light airs is not yacht racing and that it should continue to be prohibited. At the same time, it is common to hear statements that nobody knows what the rule means. In a number of important regattas, the judges have observed clear cases of pumping and rocking in the first race and have disqualified one or more boats for infringing rule 60. When this has occurred, there has been little if any further problem with pumping, ooching or rocking during the rest of the series, which indicates that competitors do in fact know what constitutes pumping, ooching and rocking and when these activities are prohibited and when they (other than rocking) may legitimately be used, and have acted accordingly. This leads to the conclusion that the problem is not with the rule itself, but with its observance by competitors and its enforcement by competitors and by protest committees and judges. Criteria to assist in the enforcement are indicated above.'

Although this American interpretation is lengthy, it is precise and comprehensive, and should provide invaluable guidance to competitors and race committees alike.

Coming, now, to more recent events, the first race for the International Finn class at Weymouth Olympic Week 1980 was sailed in light airs, and it was observed by two members of the protest committee as the boats rounded the windward mark for the second time, that is from a beat to a run. These two members reported to the race committee that some 30 seconds and about 75 metres after rounding the mark, they watched the masts of three boats, which they identified, very obviously

rocking from side to side rhythmically and persistently, in marked contrast to the masts of other nearby boats. The two members, using a stopwatch and a tape recorder, recorded one boat doing 15 rocks, after which she continued rocking, and they observed the other two boats acting similarly.

In accordance with rule 70.2(a) (Action by Race or Protest Committee—With a Hearing), the protest committee summoned the three boats to attend a meeting at which the evidence, consisting of counting the rocks recorded on tape, was played. This was the deciding factor in disqualifying two of the three boats under rule 60.2. As the third boat had already been disqualified under rule 70.1(a) for failing to start correctly, the race committee

**Plate 28**   The roll tack is something which springs to mind at the very mention of rule 60 (Means of Propulsion). Roll tacking is quite legal, provided that it does not increase a yacht's speed, after completing her tack, beyond that at which she was travelling before she tacked. But excessive roll tacking is not legal; who is to decide what is excessive?                                                                                     *William Rowntree*

did not proceed further against her. As a result of this action by the race committee under rule 60.2(e), no further rocking was seen during the rest of the series, which supports the USYRU's conclusion.

*Roll-tacking.* In the case of *Picotee* v. *Gannet* (RYA 1978/4), *Gannet* was disqualified under rule 60.2(e) for frequent roll-tacking in calm and near-calm conditions. *Gannet* appealed on the ground that the race committee's decision was too narrow an interpretation of the rule, because she and witnesses stated that there were frequent changes in the true and apparent wind direction. The appeal was dismissed on the facts found.

*Checking way by abnormal means.* This provision was introduced in 1950 rule 24, Means of Propulsion, and resulted from an incident in a race in the Prince of Wales Cup for International Fourteens at Cowes in 1939; World War II accounted for the lapse of time between cause and effect.

*Thunder* (Peter—now Sir Peter—Scott and John Winter), the outside dinghy of a number in line abreast running for a mark, was deliberately slowed down as she approached the mark, by holding bailers over the side to act as brakes. She then cut across the transoms of the other dinghies and rounded the mark in second place immediately astern of the leading inside dinghy, eventually winning the race.

Two questions arose. Is it permissible: (a) to hold the water by means of a bailer or other similar contrivance; or (b) to use a drogue or other object attached to a rope, to stop a boat's way?

The YRA decided that the use of a sea anchor in an ocean race was a matter of seamanship, and (b) was permissible. But in an ordinary round-the-buoys race, if a boat uses a bailer or any means of stopping a boat in order to gain an advantage, other than by easing or pulling in sheets, or sheering from side to side with the tiller, it would be regarded as checking way by abnormal means.

In USYRU Appeal No 132, May 1970, the New York Yacht Club said that yachts had recently been built with, in effect, two rudders—one on the keel, often called a trim tab, and a principal rudder further aft. Usually these rudders can be operated either together or separately, each having its own wheel, and when turned hard in opposite directions, they would have a braking effect. The question was, would the use of opposed rudders to check way be an abnormal means of doing so? The Appeals Committee decided: 'Sails are intended to transmit power from the wind to give a vessel forward speed, but from the earliest days of square riggers they have been backed to stop forward motion. Rudders are intended to transmit power from the flow of water to change the direction of the boat and in the process, drag is increased and the boat slowed. The second rudder is intended to improve performance on some points of sailing and when so used is set at the desired angle while the principal rudder is used to steer with, sometimes being in opposition to the first rudder. Using opposed rudders hard over to slow a boat departs from the regular use only in degree and purpose and is comparable to backing sails. Under these circumstances it is held that such use to slow a boat is not abnormal means of doing so and does not infringe rule 60.

## Racing after Sunset

Few dinghy helmsmen can have had any experience of racing their vessels at night, and even those who have competed in 24-hour dinghy races cannot really claim to have raced their vessels at night under the International Regulations for Preventing Collisions at Sea.

To take an example, the West Lancashire YC sailing instructions for its annual 24-hour race merely state that from 2000 to 0600 yachts shall show simple port and starboard sidelights supplied by the club. Unlike IRPCAS Rule 25, Sailing Vessels Underway And Vessels Under Oars, the sailing instructions do not require a sternlight to be exhibited, and it is doubtful whether the lights supplied are visible at the regulation minimum range of one mile or comply with the appropriate IMO technical requirements appended to the IRPCAS.

Futhermore, the sailing instructions do not comply with IYRU rule 3.2(b)(ii) (The Sailing Instructions), which requires them to state, when the race is to continue after sunset, the time at which the IRPCAS shall replace the corresponding rules of Part IV. They are silent on this point.

Having attended this event once or twice, I know that numerous collisions occur at night without acknowledgement of fault and, had the IRPCAS been in force, the number of rule infringements would probably have been doubled.

However, for helmsmen who compete in races that continue after sunset and become bound by the IRPCAS, the case of *Star Song* v. *Stampede* (Appeal Case No. 54, 1976, of the Canadian Yachting Association) provides some useful guidance.

What happened in this case was that, at about 0030, two yachts L and W were running on starboard tack on parallel courses some two lengths apart; L was just clear ahead of W, which was to windward and steadily closing up on L.

In accordance with IYRU rule 3.2(b)(ii), the sailing instructions prescribed that the IRPCAS replaced the corresponding rules of Part IV.

L altered course to starboard and forced W to respond to avoid a collision. W protested against L under Part B, Steering And Sailing Rules, Section II, Conduct of vessels in sight of one another, Rule 17(a)(i), Action by stand-on vessel, of the IRPCAS, on the grounds that 'luffing was forbidden at night.

The race committee upheld W's protest and imposed a five-per-cent time penalty on L. L appealed against this decision, claiming that the facts found by the race committee were incorrect and that it had misapplied the relevant IRPCAS rules.

The Appeals Committee disallowed the appeal, commenting on its decision as follows:

'It seems to be a generally-accepted principle among yachtsmen that 'luffing is not permitted after dark'. Few seem to know the rule or rules governing such behaviour and the Appeals Committee feels it to be worthwhile to

expand on these matters for the future guidance of racing yachts and race committees.

It must first be emphasized that the IRPCAS are intended to ensure the safety of vessels at sea, by precluding situations which might lead to a collision. They should not be construed as substitute rules for racing. Defined yacht racing terms such as 'luffing', 'overlap', 'proper course', and so on should not, therefore, be used in conjunction with these IRPCAS rules in order to decide a protest.

'In the above case, W was the overtaking vessel. IRPCAS Rule 13(b) states:

> A vessel shall be deemed to be overtaking when coming up with another vessel from a direction more than 22.5 degrees abaft her beam, that is, in such a position with reference to the vessel she is overtaking, that at night she would be able to see only the sternlight of that vessel but neither of her sidelights.

Rule 13(d) states:

> Any subsequent alteration of bearing between the two vessels shall not make the overtaking vessel a crossing vessel within the meaning of these Rules or relieve her of the duty of keeping clear of the overtaken vessel until she is finally past and clear.

The duties of an overtaking vessel are given in Rule 13(a):

> Notwithstanding anything contained in the Rules of this Section any vessel overtaking any other shall keep out of the way of the vessel being overtaken.

However, the overtaken vessel, in this case L, does herself have obligations towards the overtaking vessel. These are spelled out in Rule 17(a)(i);

> Where one of two vessels is to keep out of the way the other shall keep her course and speed.

Futher, Rule 17(b) states:

> When, from any cause, the vessel required to keep her course and speed finds herself so close

that collision cannot be avoided by the action of the give-way vessel alone, she shall take such action as will best aid to avoid collision.

'It is Rule 17(a)(i) which effectively prevents, in these circumstances the racing manoeuvre known as 'luffing'. Therefore, while W was in near proximity to L, neither vessel was permitted to make a course alteration which would require the other to be ready to respond in order to avoid a collision. Acting upon the facts found by the protest committee, the appeal is, therefore, disallowed and the decision to penalize L is upheld.

'It should, perhaps be emphasized that the IRPCAS do not describe situations so precisely as do the IYRU racing rules; thus the phrase 'near proximity' used above does not refer to any exact distance, (e.g., two boat-lengths), but must be taken in the context of whatever precautions to avoid a collision appear to be seamanlike under the prevailing circumstances.'

Race committees and helmsmen should be grateful to the CYA Appeals Committee for the trouble it took in so clearly setting out the reasons for its decision, in what is almost the only published case concerning the application of the IRPCAS to a yacht racing situation.

## Boardsailing

All of this book is generally speaking applicable to boardsailing. However, since this branch of the sport is relatively young and rapidly expanding, the rules under which it is conducted must be capable of being modified to suit its own peculiarities. The sheer numbers involved, for example, far exceed previous statistics under the International Yacht Racing Rules: at least 500,000 boards are in use in the Mistral, Windglider and Windsurfer classes, of which the Windglider was adopted by the IYRU Permanent Committee in 1980 as the Olympic class for the 1984 Olympic Regatta at Los Angeles.

In the sport's early stages, some of its pioneers believed that it would be necessary to

make a number of radical departures from the well-established principles of yacht racing. However, further experience and study seem to indicate that relatively few changes are required. The 1981-4 Rules lists those already adopted, in its Appendix 2 (Sailboard Racing Rules) reproduced below, but the following

**Plate 29** Sailboard 310 ranked as a capsized yacht from the moment her masthead touched the water until her masthead was lifted from the water (Appendix 2, Definition 1.2(a)). As such, rule 46.1 required Sailboard 347 to keep clear of her. However, 310 ranks as a yacht which is either tacking or gybing from the moment (as in this photograph) her masthead is lifted from the water until her sail is out of the water and it has filled (Appendix 2, Definition 1.2(b)). As such, rule 41.1 requires that she shall then keep clear of 347, which is a yacht on a tack. This means that a sailboard should not try to recover from a capsize if she may be caught with her masthead lifted from the water but before the sail is out of the water and filled – during that period, the recovering sailboard is most vulnerable, as she has to keep clear but has no way on. It is thus better to wait with masthead in the water (so that others have to keep clear), until an uninterrupted recovery can be assured.                                        *Colin Jarman*

points may also need consideration in the future:

1. The standard five-minute intervals between the warning, preparatory and starting signals may be reduced to 3-2-0 minutes, because competitors dislike being forced to sail about in the vicinity of the starting line for so long in either light or heavy weather conditions. This is no problem because in the early stages of the RYA Team Championship, the sailing instructions prescribe that the starting signals will be made at intervals of two minutes.

2. It is becoming accepted that the strict application of 720° Turns (Alternative Penalty) is the only practicable method of conducting these events, otherwise the resulting spate of protests would overwhelm any number of protest committees. This accounts for the fact that to date the RYA RRC has not been required to adjudicate on any boardsailing appeal.

3. Further experience may suggest that owing to the speeds of the boards, the two-lengths determinative of rule 42.3 (a) may need to be extended. At one time, the catamarans contemplated asking the IYRU to make a similar amendment for their races, but to date they have not proceeded with this.


## APPENDIX 2 – Sailboard Racing Rules

*For the period 1981-1984 the IYRU will permit annual changes to Appendix 2 to be approved and implemented at each November meeting.*

A sailboard is a surfboard type vessel using a free sail system. A free sail system means a swivel mounted mast not supported in a permanent position while sailing. Sailboard races shall be sailed under the International Yacht Racing Rules modified as follows:

**1    Part 1 – Definitions**

1.1    *Leeward and Windward* – The side on which a sailboard is or was carrying her mainsail is assumed to be the side on which she would carry her mainsail in order to make progress forward ignoring mast heeling.

1.2    *Capsize* –
   (a) A sailboard shall rank as a *capsized* yacht from the moment her masthead touches the water until her masthead is lifted from the water.
   (b) A sailboard recovering from a *capsize* shall rank as a yacht which is either *tacking* or *gybing* from the moment her masthead is lifted from the water until her sail is out of the water and it has filled.

**2    Part III – General Requirements**

2.1    Rule 23 – Anchor
An anchor and chain or rope need not be carried.

2.2    Rule 24 – Life-Saving Equipment
Unless otherwise prescribed in the sailing instructions, a safety line shall be attached between the base of the mast(s) and the hull.

**3    Part IV – Right of Way Rules**

3.1    Rule 38.2 – Same Tack – Luffing and Sailing above a Proper Course after Starting

Rule 40 – Same Tack – Luffing before Starting
The normal station of the helmsman shall be at the aft edge of the centreboard well. For 'mainmast' read 'mastfoot'.

3.2    Capsized when Starting

Between her preparatory and starting signals a sailboard shall have her sail out of the water and in a normal position, except when capsized. She shall have the onus of satisfying the race committee that a *capsize* was unintentional and that every effort was made to recover immediately.

3.3    Sailing Backward when Starting

When approaching the starting line to *start* or when returning to the prestart side of the starting line a sailboard sailing or drifting backward shall keep clear of other sailboards or yachts which are *starting* or have *started* correctly.

## 4 Part V - Other Sailing Rules

Rule 60.1 – Means of Propulsion
Dragging a foot in the water infringes this rule.

## 5 Part VI – Protests, Penalties and Appeals

Rule 68 – Protests by Yachts
A sailboard shall not be required to display a flag in order to signify a **protest** as required by rule 68.2 but, except when rule 68.3 applies, she shall notify the other sailboard or yacht by hail at the first reasonable opportunity and the race committee as soon as possible after *finishing* or retiring.

## 6 Rules for Multi-Mast Sailboards

6.1 The mainsail is the foremost sail and the mainmast is the foremost mast.

6.2 Rule 1.2 (a) – A sailboard shall rank as a *capsized* yacht from the moment all her mastheads touch the water until one masthead is lifted from the water.

6.3 Rule 1.2 (b) – A sailboard recovering from a *capsize* shall rank as a yacht which is either *tacking* or *gybing* from the moment one masthead is lifted from the water until all her sails are out of the water and they have filled.

6.4 Rule 3.1 – The normal station of the helmsman is the normal station of the crew member controlling the mainsail.

6.5 Rule 3.2 – For 'sail' read 'sails'.

## 7 Recommended Procedure for Sailboard Races

7.1 When so prescribed in the sailing instructions a sailboard race will consist of several heats: each heat to be started shortly after the preceding one has finished. A suitable time limit for each heat is between 45 and 60 minutes.

7.2 Each heat shall be started in accordance with rule 4.4 (Signals), however the interval between the signals for starting a race may be reduced.

7.3 The race committee shall be notified of retirement or intention to protest as soon as possible after each heat. Further requirements for lodging a **protest** shall be fulfilled after the race in accordance with rules 68.5, 68.6, 68.7 and 68.8. (Protests by Yachts).

*Questions*

**Q8.1** Two yachts racing anchor; one drags her anchor so that the two yachts make contact. Which is in the wrong?

**Q8.2** Which yacht has right of way under:
  (a) IYRU rules?
  (b) IRPCAS?

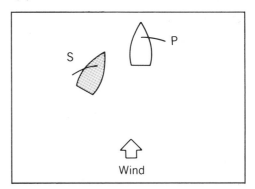

**Fig. Q8.2**

**Q8.3** Five minutes after the situation shown in question 8.2 above, the situation is as now shown. Who has right of way under IRPCAS?

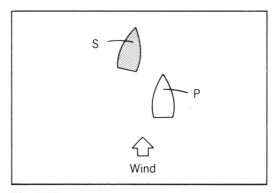

**Fig. Q8.3**

# 9 Protests and Appeals

## Definition of Protest

The word 'protest' in its nautical meaning of a declaration requires some further explanation. Too many of today's sailors consider it to be the action of a disgruntled skipper protesting against the rules – akin to its modern connotation ashore.

Layton's *Dictionary of Nautical Words and Terms* defines it as follows:
'Protest –statement under oath, made before a notary public, concerning an actual or anticipated loss, damage or hindrance in the carrying out of a marine adventure.' Dixon Kemp defined it as: 'Protest – a declaration that a yacht has not conformed to the sailing rules; also a term used by the Commissioner of Works in case of a wreck being reported.'

When the racing rules were revised in 1977, an effort was made to find an alternative word, but none was considered suitable. In the present rules, apart from meaning a written allegation that another yacht has infringed a rule, it also encompasses redress and hearing; see IYRR Part VI – Protests, Penalties and Appeals for full definition.

## Displaying a Protest Flag

Two unusual protests relating to the application of what is now rule 68.2(a) (Protests by Yachts), occurred during the 1979 Weymouth Olympic Week.

The first arose in the International Star class, where E6356 protested against K6290 while rounding the windward mark. E6356 said she displayed flag 'B' from her port shroud immediately after beginning the ensuing run.

The helmsman and crew of K6290, and the helmsman of K6123 who protested against both the other yachts, said that they had not seen a protest flag displayed by E6356.

On being called to give evidence, the chairman of the WOW committee (who watched the finish from his inflatable) and the race officer who timed the finishes, both said they had not seen E6356 displaying a protest flag, but the race officer agreed that, after she had finished, E6356 notified him that she intended to protest; she admitted that the protest flag could have slipped down the shroud.

On this evidence, the protest committee refused E6356's protest, on the grounds that rule 68.2(a) requires a protesting yacht to display a protest flag 'conspicuously' and to keep it displayed until she finishes, which requirement the protest committee was not satisfied that E6356 had met.

The second protest occurred in the International Tornado class. K298 protested against K293, and stated on her protest form that she did not display a protest flag until ten minutes after the incident, but while still on the same leg of the course.

When K298 was asked whether the delay in displaying a protest flag resulted either from a reluctance to lose a tactical advantage, or from the danger of capsizing if the crew came inboard off his trapeze to find and display a protest flag, she admitted that the first reason was the deciding factor.

The protest committee pointed out that rule 68.2(a) required a protesting yacht to display a protest flag 'at the first reasonable opportunity.' The protest committee explained that past case law had established that a dinghy which had sailed a complete windward leg in heavy weather before displaying a protest flag had had her protest accepted, because she had satisfied the race committee that if her crew had tried to display a protest flag earlier, she would have been in danger of capsizing. In the present case, K298's protest was refused, because the protest committee was not satisfied that she displayed a protest flag at the first reasonable opportunity.

# Appeals

The RYA deals with about 50 appeals and questions from clubs each year, and when that number is related to the numbers of classes and the yachts racing in them all over the UK, it is a very small number indeed. However, in addition, the RYA refuses to adjudicate on others because the appellants either have not read or have not understood three important rules concerning the submission of appeals.

The first rule 74.1 (Finding of Facts) reads:

> The **protest committee** shall determine the facts and base its decision upon them. The finding of facts shall be final.

The second rule 77.1 (Right of Appeal) reads:

> ... the following appeals ... may be made to the national authority concerned:
> (a) a yacht which is a **party to a protest** may appeal against a decision of a **protest committee;**

The third is rule 77.3 (Interpretation of Rules) that reads:

> An appeal ... shall be made solely on a question of interpretation of the **rules**. A national authority shall accept the **protest committee's** findings of fact except that when it is not satisfied with the facts presented it may, when practicable, request further information or return the case to **the protest committee** for a re-hearing.

Hence, in order to avoid making vain and costly appeals that cause protest committees, the RYA secretariat and the Racing Rules Committee to waste a great deal of valuable time in preparing and studying them, it is essential that any prospective appellant carefully distinguishes between what in the decision of a protest is a statement of fact found and what is an interpretation of a rule. For example, when a protest committee finds as facts: 'L and W were both close-hauled on port tack; that L was one length to leeward and one length clear ahead of W; and that L then tacked to starboard' those facts are final and it is useless to appeal against them, even though L may insist that she was two lengths to leeward of W. If she does appeal, the RYA will dismiss it and L will forfeit her appeal fee.

Another important procedural point is that an appellant must forward his appeal and all his statements through the organising authority under which the race was sailed; he must not appeal direct to the national authority. There is, however, on exception to this restriction. Certain clubs do their utmost to discourage parties to protests from appealing, and some even go so far as to fail to comply with rule 77 and the RYA prescription to rule 77.1, i.e., they do not forward appeals lodged with them to the RYA. To overcome such gross misconduct, the RYA has produced an Appeal Form which the appellant can complete, sending the first part to the RYA and the second part to the organizing authority. This notifies both bodies that an appeal is being lodged. If the organising authority fails to forward the appeal to the RYA within the prescribed time limit of two months, the RYA will ask the organising authority to explain why it has not done so.

It is not always easy to decide what is a finding of fact and what is an interpretation of a rule, so a race committee must not refuse to forward an appeal to the RYA because it believes it relates only to a finding of fact. Indeed, arising from a recent appeal, the RYA RRC proposed that a prescription be added at the next opportunity to rule 77.3 as follows:

> The RYA prescribes that: All appeals shall be forwarded by the organising authority or the race committee to the RYA. The RYA will decide whether or not the appeal is a question of interpretation.

## Gross Infringements

When the Cumberland Fleet (1775-1823) (the predecessor of the Royal Thames Yacht Club) raced on the Thames off the Adelphi and Vauxhall Gardens, conditions were pretty tough. *The Morning Chronicle* of July 19th, 1786 reported:

> 'There was an attempt of foul play against the *Prince of Wales*, the winning vessel of 1786, by other boats getting in her way, but she got all clear by liberal use of handspikes'

*The Times* of July 23rd, 1975, recorded:

> The *Mercury*, which was the leading boat, somehow got foul of the *Vixen*, whereupon the captain of the *Vixen* cut away the rigging of the *Mercury* with a cutlass and fairly well dismantled her, the *Mermaid* winning the cup.'

However, in the modern sense, yacht racing as an organised sport in English waters can hardly be said to date from much earlier than 1826, when the Royal Yacht Club at Cowes, as it was then styled (now the Royal Yacht Squadron), presented a £100 Gold Cup for competition between vessels owned by its members. From then on, the sport was strongly patronised by the aristocracy and gentry, and consequently yacht clubs, and yacht owners built up a tradition of sportsmanlike behaviour afloat and ashore.

When the Yacht Racing Association formulated its first racing rules, this code of conduct was epitomised in the first rule in the book which read in part:

> *Management of races.* 1.
> All races, and all yachts sailing therein, shall be under the direction of the flag officers or sailing committee of the club under whose auspices the races are being sailed. All matters shall be subject to their approval and control, and all doubts, questions and disputes which may arise shall be subject to their decision. Their decisions shall be based upon these rules so far as they will apply, but as no rules can be devised capable of meeting every incident and accident of sailing, the sailing committee should keep in view the ordinary customs of the sea, and discourage all attempts to win a race by other means than fair sailing and superior speed and skill . . .

The importance of the sportsmanlike sentiments this rule contains cannot be overestimated. From it anybody may judge it to be perfectly obvious that every helmsman in a race must observe them, and anyone who fails to do so should be disqualified. Bluffing, or sharp practice, or lying in any shape or form are foreign to the whole spirit of the rules. One of the most dignified pronouncements of the council occured in the case of *Jade* and *Bluebell* (YRA 1936/3), when it was observed:

> 'The rules are not based upon comtemplation of misuse. No attempt whatever is made to prevent misuse because it is almost unknown. Rule 1 is sufficient should there occur isolated instances of misuse.'

The original rule 1 has been replaced in a somewhat emasculated form by the present Fundamental Rule – Fair Sailing, which supports its sentiments.

Although there is little doubt that our racing progenitors of that time sailed hard – when on starboard tack they were quite prepared to sail straight through an opponent on port tack, regardless of the consequences – with very few exceptions, they played the game in strict accordance with the letter of the law and the spirit of rule 1 above.

In 1957 I wrote in the fifth edition of my book *Yacht Racing*:

'. . . only twice since its foundation in 1875, has the RYA ever had occasion to censure a professional skipper or an amateur helmsman for foul sailing, and there is no instance in the archives of the Association of the penalty – under what is now rule 75 (Penalties for Gross Infringements of Rules or Misconduct) – ever having been put into force. This is a record of which all yachtsmen may well be proud, and it is one which every one of us should be zealous in upholding.'

Unfortunately, the statement is no longer true. In recent years there has been a lamentable decline in sporting standards generally and, alas, this decline is becoming increasingly manifest in yacht racing in principal events, not only in rule observance, but also in those standards of behaviour that distinguish gentlemen and sportsmen – both dirty words nowa-days – from cads and louts.

It is distasteful and depressing to believe it necessary to describe some gross infringements of the rules, sportsmanship and good manners that have been committed by what is hoped to be still only a small percentage of competitors. Nevertheless these comments may, on the one hand, show race committees that the IYRU racing rules empower them to proceed against such offenders and, on the other hand, warn offenders that race committees need not toler-ate such misconduct.

Shortly before the adoption of the 1973 IYRU racing rules, a number of hitherto un-known instances of misconduct by competitors had been reported. In one case, the party to a protest who had been disqualified showed his disapproval of the protest committee's decision by subsequently assaulting the chairman and knocking him out. In another case a competi-tor, at the start, demonstrated his perfectly justified objection to a number of his oppo-nents' blatant disregard of the rules by, quite unjustifiably, hitting one of them with a pad-dle, for which he was censured and suspended for a period from racing by the RYA. In other cases rigging screws and rudder pintles had been partially sawn through, so that under stress they broke and disabled the boats.

Consequently, in trying to put a stop to such inexcusable behaviour, the IYRU added a provision in 1973 to what is now rule 75.2 (Penalty for Gross Infringement of Rules or Misconduct), as follows:

> After a gross breach of good manners or sportsmanship the race committee may ex-clude a competitor either from further parti-cipation in a series or from the whole series or take other disciplinary action.

A well-known yacht racing commentator derided this new rule, but further instances of misconduct show that race committees need to be able to combat them. Soon after the adop-tion of this rule, two cases were reported, to what is now the USYRU, of helmsmen using vituperative language vehemently against other competitors. In both cases the rule was invoked, the helmsmen were penalised by several months' suspension from racing or club use or both, and their behaviour was given some publicity. Subsequently, the Australian Yachting Federation and some European national authorities reported to the IYRU suspensions of competitors for misconduct.

In the case of *Al Quadus* v Race Committee (RYA 1977/12), after the AGM of a national class held during its championship week, a competitor in a loud voice made defamatory remarks about the integrity and ability of the flag officers and race committee of the club under whose burgee the event was being sailed.

These officials took strong exception to the competitor's behaviour and regarded his re-marks as slanderous. Feeling that they had been publicly insulted, they sought an apology through the class secretary, making it clear that unless it was forthcoming before the next day's race, the competitor would be excluded from the club under the rules of its constitution that dealt with conduct prejudicial to its in-terests, and he would then be ineligible to race under its burgee.

The race committee resolved that if the competitor did not apologise and sailed in the next day's race, his presence in it would be ignored. No apology was made and the com-petitor sailed in the next race. His yacht was therefore recorded in the results as DSQ.

The competitor's appeal was dismissed. In its decision, the RYA gave some useful gui-dance on how to deal with a gross infringement of the IYRU racing rules, the sailing instruc-tions or the class rules, and added:

'However, no mandatory procedure is laid down as to how a race committee shall decide that there has been a gross breach of good manners or sportsmanship, not involving the IYRU racing rules, the sailing instructions or the class rules, nor does rule 75.2 place any restrictions upon the freedom of a race com-mittee to take disciplinary action.

'In the particular case, neither the alleged breach nor the appeal involve the IYRU rac-ing rules, the sailing instructions or the class rules. It is therefore a matter which may be dealt with by the race committee.

'The council sees no reason to reverse the race committee's decision and recommends that the race result sheet should be annotated: "Excluded from race under the club's rules 12.8 and 9." '

Although the RYA recommended the club to deal with this unpleasant episode as a domestic matter, the club does not seem to have known that it could have proceeded under rule 75.21. The essence of that rule is that a race committee must be able to show an offender the door immediately, just as one would be entitled to do in one's own house. Neither the host (club), nor the guests (competitors) should have to put up with anyone who behaves in this way.

In the handling of rule 75.2, two kinds of question arise. In the first, an individual says or does something that is thought to be an infringement of the rule, and the question is, how much of the story is fact, and how much is opinion as to whether or not the act is a gross breach of good manners or sportsmanship? The two tend to become combined into one, but they need to be separated.

The second question is what constitutes a gross breach? It is quite easy for a race committee to feel that a little excessive exuberance is a gross breach, or to put it another way, that what in the pressure of the moment is considered to be a gross breach, in a calm mood at a distance is simply a breach. But because the word breach is not defined – and it would not be easy to define it – it seems that the right of appeal in these cases is one that should be supported, and it would do no harm to let it come up to an appeals committee once in a while and give it a chance to interpret the rule and support the race committee. Probably only a small percentage of such decisions would be appealed anyway, and when one is, appeals take some time to be decided, and meanwhile the penalty is probably being imposed on the individual, and that is not all bad either in a case of this sort, even if it is not a gross breach.

The Norwegian Yachting Association submitted Appeal No. 1/1975 to the IYRU for approval as an Interpretation, and it is now Case 78. The facts were that, after five races of

a championship series of six races, the points scored by A were such that she was bound to win the event, regardless of her own finishing position in the sixth race, provided that B did not finish ahead of her among the first three yachts. There were 48 competitors.

A started prematurely in the sixth race and was recalled. She responded after sailing about 70 metres away from the starting line, but sailed only about 30 metres towards it when she met B which had started correctly. A then turned and sailed on top of B, harassing her throughout the first windward leg, so that A rounded the windward mark last-but-one, and B rounded it last. A then retired and B subsequently finished 22nd.

On this basis, the race committee further established that A continued to race, despite her knowing that she had started prematurely, and that she did so solely for the purpose of harassing B. The race committee disqualified A for failing to return and start correctly and for infringing rule 33.1 (Rule Infringement), and the Fundamental Rule – Fair Sailing.

A discarded this race, won the championship and then appealed against her disqualification under the last rule, asserting that she thought she had returned and started correctly.

The appeals committee dismissed the appeal and said that the facts showed gross infringements of the rules and of sportsmanship. Such deliberate attempts at winning a series by unfair means should be strongly discouraged. To disqualify A in the sixth race only was not enough, since she would then have achieved the purpose of the unfair action and would have won the championship.

Rule 75.2 and in particular the last part of that rule, can be applied to exclude A from the whole series. Such exclusion, in the opinion of the committee, was within the meaning of the words 'other disciplinary action', and this interpretation of the rule is certainly in the spirit of the racing rules.

A was excluded from the whole series, and all her results struck from the list of results as if she had not started in any of the races.

In accepting this case as an Interpretation,

the IYRU endorsed the NYA's Appeals Committee's decision. Obviously, A did not win the series by fair sailing as required by the Fundamental Rule – Fair Sailing, since she attacked B by deliberately disregarding any possibility of winning that race herself. Such behaviour can legitimately be regarded as a gross breach of sportsmanship, and hence is appropriately penalisable under rule 75.2. In addition, race committees should know that IYRU rule 1.3 (Authority for Organising Conducting and Judging Races), entitles them, if they so wish, not only to rescind an entry, but to refuse to accept any future entry from an offender.

Naturally, no club would want to be forced to take any of these punitive measures but, because of the comparative rarity of the kinds of misconduct described, many clubs may not know that they have these powers, and some publicity may dissuade certain less civilised competitors from committing such offences.

Two more points, and this distasteful subject can be closed. First, some time ago a successful board sailor wrote an article in one of the yachting periodicals advising readers how to win races. Many of his recommendations were in direct opposition to the whole traditions and principles of yacht racing that have been discussed. For example, he wrote, 'You've got to be aggressive, angry even.' He had the grace to admit that some actions he advocated were 'really rather naughty and in some cases clear breaches of the rules' – an understatement if ever there was one – and he assumed that he was at liberty to indulge in 'a screaming tirade of obscenities at a back marker' who at a critical moment inadvertently gets in the way. It is understood that he has since seen the error of his ways and now much regrets his remarks. Nevertheless, while it is a relief to know that he has changed his mind, if his original attitude exemplified that of some of the up-and-coming sailors, the outlook is grim.

Secondly, the amount of lying by parties to protests in principal events is steadily increasing. Although due allowance must be made for language difficulties, differing degrees of awareness, perception and recollection of helmsmen and crews when giving evidence, and differing understanding of the rules, the fact remains that some will lie unashamedly to try to avoid disqualification. At a recent European class championship, the jury, being satisfied that false evidence was given by one of the parties, quite rightly proceeded against the offender under Fundamental Rule – Fair Sailing and rule 75.2, and excluded him from the series, which action was upheld by the national authority concerned.

Bryan Willis – chairman of the jury for the Laser European Championship at Lemvig, Denmark, in July 1980 – reported to the RYA RRC that three competitors had been disqualified from individual races for infringing particular rules, and had also been excluded from the whole series under the Fundamental Rule – Fair Sailing, and what is now rule 75.2. Two of them had lied and the third had cheated.

In an article entitled 'Lying at a Protest Hearing', published in the magazine *Dinghy and Board Sailing*, September 1980, Bryan Willis said that one of the most useful pieces of equipment in which the Laser Association had invested was a fairly simple and inexpensive black-and -white video tape recorder. This had proved invaluable, in that it clearly showed two of the above competitors infringing those rules that they had been alleged to have broken and which, after having been warned that it was a serious offence to lie, they had denied breaking.

## Requesting Redress

Certain requests for redress by yachts during the 1980 Weymouth Olympic Week were decided by the protest committee and, before describing them, it may be helpful to discuss the applicable rules.

Incidentally, the term protest committee is used throughout this section, but the term international jury also applies. The distinction between the two is that decisions of a protest committee are subject to appeal, whereas those of an international jury are not. To qualify for the latter status, a jury's composition must comply with Appendix 8 (Terms of Reference and Conditions for its Decisions to be Final).

The sole difference between the two procedures is that, although in both cases yachts must observe rule 68.5 (Particulars to be Included), rule 69 (Requests for Redress) states that a yacht requesting redress need not display a protest flag.

In this connection, the first point to note – although perhaps somewhat pedantic – is that according to rule 68.1 (Protests by Yachts), a yacht can protest against any other yacht; rule 69 refers to a yacht requesting redress from a protest committee. The reason for this distinction is that, when revising the rules in 1965, the IYRU decided that to protest against that hard-working body, which usually gets more brickbats than bouquets, showed disrespect and lack of appreciation of its labours!

Secondly, although for many years it had been taken for granted that a yacht could protest when she believed that her chances of winning a prize had been prejudiced by an action of the race committee, the rules were silent on this point until, in 1950, the IYRU adopted rule 38.5(a) – now rule 69 in a slightly modified form. There are many ways in which a race committee's action or omission may prejudice a yacht's finishing position – no longer limited to 'her chances of winning a prize'. For example, issuing misleading or ambiguous sailing instructions; late changes of course; errors in the timing of starting signals; oral instructions; recall numbers displayed too late or removed too soon; shortening course signals made too late; errors in yachts' finishing times or order; and improper protest procedure, to mention some of the points relating to the proper management of races.

Although rule 1.2 (Authority for Organising, Conducting and Judging Races) invests the race committee with full authority, rule 1.4 enjoins that its authority must be exercised in accordance with the rules as a whole so, when it makes a mistake that materially prejudices a yacht's finishing position, rule 69 entitles her to request redress from the protest committee and, if she is then dissatisfied with its decision, she can appeal.

In addition to the options now listed in rule 74.2 (Consideration of Redress) that are open to the protest committee, the case of *Francessa* v Race Committee (RYA 1968/14; IYRU Case 38) – in which that yacht went to the assistance of a capsized competitor – occurred under 1965 rule 12, which was the same as in 1961. Hence the decision of this case specified some 'other arrangements' that could be utilised.

This stated:

Depending on the circumstances, such an arrangement could, in appropriate conditions, include the following:

(a) To arrange a sail-off between the prejudiced yacht and those which at the time were ahead of or close to her, if they could be identified.

(b) To award the prejudiced yacht breakdown points.

(c) If the incident occurred close enough to the finishing line for the race committee to determine with some certainty her probable finishing position, to award her the points she would have obtained had she finished in that position.

(d) In accordance with Appendix 5 – Olympic Scoring System, para. 3, to award her points equal to the average to the nearest tenth of a point, of her points in all races in the series, except the race in question and her worst race, when a discard is allowed.'

Two other possible options could be either to award points according to her position at the last rounding mark before the incident if the rounding order had been recorded or, in a single race for prizes (assuming that she could qualify for one), to follow part of the decision in the case of the Dar-es-Salaam Yacht Club (RYA 1961/3), which said:

'Where a race committee makes an unfortunate mistake and therby causes a yacht to be placed at a disadvantage, the usual custom has been to give an additional prize to the vessel so affected (Tranmere Sailing Club, YRA 1900).'

All these options are mentioned because race committees, faced with the need to grant redress, sometimes take the easy way out and abandon or cancel the race, without regard for the effect of its decision on the rest of the fleet that completed the course correctly in accordance with the rules. These two options are placed at the bottom of the list because only as a last resort should either be adopted, and then only subject to the proviso.

Rule 58 requires any yacht while racing to render all possible assistance to any vessel or person in peril, even when either may have nothing whatever to do with the race in question.

When, by turning aside to observe this universally-accepted humanitarian custom of the sea, a yacht not responsible for the emergency prejudices her finishing position, she is entitled to request redress. It may be that as a result she is passed by other yachts in the race which may have been too far away to notice the incident and are genuinely ignorant of the fact that help was needed, or they arrive after the emergency has been dealt with, and continue in the race. It should be noted that rule 58 has been relaxed to the extent that when a yacht fails to render assistance, if in the view of the race committee it was unnecessary for her to do so, she need not *ipso facto* be disqualified. For example, in a race in which a rescue launch is standing by a capsized boat and another boat nearby does not alter course to see whether any further assistance is required, it would be for the race committee, after hearing the evidence, to decide whether or not to disqualify her.

Obviously, it would be most unfair to a yacht that had rendered assistance if virtue were unrewarded and she were unable to seek redress. However, the race committee's power to act under rule 74.2(c) is discretionary and not mandatory. For example, when a yacht at the back of the fleet in a single race without a time allowance renders assistance, her finishing position would hardly be materially prejudiced, and the race committee would be justified in letting the results of the race stand.

With regard to rule 69(c), which enables a yacht to request redress when she has been disabled by another that should have kept clear, the above principles also apply.

When damage results from such a collision, the case of the Salcombe Yacht Club (RYA 1968/2; IYRU Case 36) makes the point that

in determining whether or not the damage is serious, consideration must be given to its extent and whether it was feasible or prudent for the damaged yacht to continue racing and, if so, whether the damage markedly affected her speed and materially prejudiced her finishing position. For instance, a collision might break a rigging link of a mast stepped on deck, causing it to fall overboard and disable the yacht, the actual extent of the damage being negligible. Moreover, even though she might have effected a repair, the time taken to recover the mast on board and fix the shroud securely would almost certainly have materially prejudiced her finishing position.

Although the majority of requests for redress are *bona fide* and based on a race committee's error, sadly there is a growing tendency for some yachts that have performed poorly in a race to invoke rule 69 in an attempt to persuade the race committee either to re-sail the race and give them a chance of doing better, or to award them average points for various dubious reasons. Race committees should therefore beware of such try-ons.

The IYRU RRC interpreted the phrase 'being disabled' in rule 69(c), (Requests for Redress), (1982 Yearbook p. 74) as follows:

'A disabled yacht is one that is damaged to such an extent that she cannot proceed either at her normal speed or cannot proceed in safety. A yacht whose finishing position is "materially prejudiced" by an incident, but not "disabled", cannot request redress under this rule.'

Having dealt with the theoretical aspects of rule 69, let us turn to their practical application to the requests for redress by competitors from the WOW protest committee of 1980.

First, after two general recalls and the imposition of the five-minute disqualification rule between the warning and preparatory signals for the restart of a 470 race, a windshift caused the starting line to become biassed. In a well-intentioned but mistaken effort to rectify this, the race officer ordered the port-end starting line mark to be shifted to windward to provide a fair start. Unfortunately the mark was not relaid in the new position until some thirty seconds after the preparatory signal had been made, thus infringing rule 4.3 (a) (Changing the Course), which reads:

> The course for a class which has not started may be changed:–
>
> (a) when the only change is that a starting *mark* may be shifted, by shifting the *mark* before the preparatory signal is made . . .

18 out of a total of 40 starters made premature starts and were disqualified, two of which requested redress on the grounds that they had carefully checked the original position of the mark by noting shore transits. They claimed that shifting the mark was an act of the race committee which materially prejudiced their starts, and led to their making premature starts and subsequent disqualification, and asked for the race to be re-sailed.

The race officer, acting as the agent of the race committee, said that when the mark was relaid four-and-a-half minutes before the starting signal, no yachts were anywhere near the starting line; that the group of premature starters crossed the starting line during the last 30 seconds before the starting signal; and that in his opinion the effect of shifting the mark was negligible.

The protest committee then said that before proceeding further, it had to satisfy itself that the decision it reached was as equitable as possible to all yachts concerned, by taking appropriate evidence: that is from the yachts that had started correctly and finished in the first three places.

These three yachts said that they had carefully avoided making premature starts and had observed the rules while racing. Very naturally, they saw no justification for abandoning and re-sailing the race and depriving them of their places and points, which view represented that of the rest of the fleet.

USYRU Appeal No. 201 (1977) says, in part:
'The application of rule 69 is a three-step process: 1. Did the race committee commit an error:? 2. If so, was any yacht materially prejudiced? 3. If so, what action under rule 74.2 can be taken by way of compensation for a yacht or yachts materially prejudiced, which will be as equitable as possible to all competitors. The third step can be taken only when the answers to both the first two questions are in the affirmative.'

In the WOW case, the race committee made two errors. First it changed the course after the preparatory signal, contrary to rule 4.3(a). When the race officer saw that the mark was relaid too late, he should, secondly, have signalled N over X and fired three guns, indicating that the race was abandoned and would shortly be re-sailed. This would have caused further delay, but would have enabled the race officer to have re-started the race correctly and obviated any complaint.

The protest committee, while accepting that the race committee infringed rule 4.3 (a), concluded that this did not materially prejudice any yacht or yachts and supported the views of the three placed yachts and decided to let the results of the race stand.

The second request for redress was made by a Tornado, in the hope of being awarded average points, because before the start her forestay fitting broke, thus preventing her from competing in the race. As rule 69 makes no provision for the damage she suffered and excludes gear failure resulting from poor design or maintenance, the request was refused.

The third request for redress was submitted by one of the two Swedish Tornados racing at Weymouth. The grounds were that she was one of the first Tornados to leave the beach but, instead of sailing direct to the committee boat to check the signals, she chose to sail well to windward of the starting area to study the conditions on the first windward leg of the course. She finally gybed and sailed towards the starting-line, during which time the warning signal was made and, as she was still on the course side of the line when the one-minute round-the-ends rule came into effect, she had no chance of making a fair start and was thus prevented from racing against the other Swedish Tornado. This was important to her because the results of the series decided which of the two would be selected to represent Sweden in the Olympic regatta.

The protest committee, while appreciating her situation, decided that her finishing position was not in any way prejudiced by an action or omission of the race committee and refused her request.

Finally, a yacht in the Star class asked for average points to be awarded her on the grounds that her crew had been called away to deal with some business matter, and therefore she was unable to start in that day's race.

The three headings of rule 69 under which redress could be requested were read to the claimant, and he was asked under which of them redress was being requested. He replied that he thought the protest committee had special powers to deal with such a situation! The request was refused as none of the provisions of that rule was applicable.

The following are the two principal rules quoted in this section:

### 69      Requests for Redress

A yacht which alleges that her finishing position has been materially prejudiced through no fault of her own by:

(a) an action or omission of the race committee, or

(b) rendering assistance in accordance with rule 58, (Rendering Assistance), or

(c) being disabled by another vessel which was required to keep clear.

may request redress from the **protest committee** in accordance with the requirements for a **protest** provided in rules 68.5, 68.6, 68.7 and 68.8. (Protests by Yachts). A protest flag need not be displayed. The **protest committee** shall then proceed in accordance with rule 74.2. (Consideration of Redress).

### 74.2      CONSIDERATION OF REDRESS

(a) When consideration of redress has been initiated as provided in rule 69, (Requests for Redress), or rule 70.3. (Yacht Materially Prejudiced), the **protest committee** shall decide whether the finishing position of a yacht or yachts has been materially prejudiced in any of the circumstances set out in rule 69.

(b) If so, the **protest committee** shall satisfy itself by taking appropriate evidence, especially before *abandoning* or *cancelling*

the race, that it is aware of the relevant facts and of the probable consequences of any arrangement, to all yachts concerned for that particular race and for the series, if any, as a whole.

(c) The **protest committee** shall then make as equitable an arrangement as possible for all yachts concerned. This may be to let the results of the race stand, to adjust the points score or the finishing time of the prejudiced yacht or to *abandon* or *cancel* the race or to adopt some other means.

## Questions

**Q9.1**   Is there any essential difference between a yacht v yacht protest, and a race committee v yacht protest?

**Q9.2**   If the procedure at a protest hearing has been incorrect, for example no written protest, how should an appeal on the grounds of incorrect procedure be dealt with when the protestor admits infringement of an applicable rule?

**Q9.3**   What are the obligations of observers appointed by the race committee to monitor rule infringements?

**Q9.4**   Can a disqualified yacht appeal against a protest committee's finding of facts?

**Q9.5**   Can a yacht appeal direct to her national authority?

**Q9.6**   Can a protest committee refuse to forward an appeal to the national authority, on the grounds that it does not concern the interpretation of a rule?

**Q9.7**   Which rules specify an onus of satisfying the protest committee?

**Q9.8**   Must a protest committee always decide a protest?

# Appendix
# Answers to Test Questions

**A1.1**  The Fundamental Rules are:
(a) Fair sailing (unnumbered).
(b) Responsibility of a yacht (unnumbered).

**A1.2**  A yacht is racing and amenable to the racing rules from her preparatory signal until she has either finished and cleared the finishing line and finishing marks, or retired, or until the race has been postponed, abandoned, cancelled, or a general recall has been signalled, unless otherwise prescribed in the sailing instructions (definition).

**A1.3**  The four basic positional relationships are:
(a) On opposite tacks; the port-tack yacht keeps clear.
(b) On the same tack; the windward yacht keeps clear.
(c) Changing tack; the tacking or gybing yacht keeps clear.
(d) One yacht is anchored, aground or capsized; the yacht under way keeps clear.

**A1.4**  No. When two yachts touch, one must retire or accept an alternative penalty when available, or one or both must protest. Only the protest committee can decide whether or not the contact was minor and unavoidable.

**A2.1**
(a) When the right-of-way yacht holds luffing rights under rule 38.1.
(b) When assuming a proper course to start. But, before she has started and cleared the starting line, she is subject to rule 40, which only allows her to luff slowly and in such a way as to give a windward yacht room and opportunity to keep clear.
(c) When rounding a mark. When she is clear ahead, she may luff, bear away or gybe, but when she has to tack to round the mark, she is subject to rule 41, which says that she must keep clear of a yacht on a tack (even though the latter is clear astern and would be the give-way yacht if there were no mark to round).

**A2.2**  Rule 41.3 makes it clear that the yacht which tacks or gybes has the onus of satisfying the race committe that she completed her tack or gybe in accordance with rule 41.2.

**A2.3**  No. The right-of-way yacht is at all times bound by rule 35 (Limitations on Altering Course) not to alter course so as to prevent the give-way yacht from keeping clear, or so as to obstruct her while she is keeping clear.

**A2.4**  Yes at any time, unless she is so close as to prevent the port-tack yacht from keeping clear, or as to obstruct her while she is trying to do so.

**A2.5**  No, because this is an opposite-tacks situation. A yacht can have luffing rights only in a same-tack situation.

**A2.6**  It means putting the give-way yacht at a disadvantage greater than that which she would have suffered in complying with her obligation, if the right-of-way yacht had held her course.

**A3.1**  No. Rule 41.2 is in Section B of the Rules, which applies except when over-ridden by a rule of Section C. S in the drawing ranks as an obstruction to PL, who is not obliged to go under her stern; PL may claim room from PW to tack at an obstruction under rule 42.1(a) of Section C. Under rule 43.1, PL must hail to this effect.

**A3.2**  If SW believes that there is room for SL

to tack and still hold a close-hauled course on port tack while SW passes safely ahead of her, SW should hail 'You tack' and hold on. The onus of proof that there was room for this to happen will lie on SW; rule 43.2(b). Otherwise SW must tack at the earliest possible moment after the hail; rule 43.2(a).

**A3.3** Rule 37.2, which requires a yacht clear astern to keep clear of a yacht clear ahead, only applies to yachts on the same tack. Rule 36 applies here, and P must keep clear as port-tack yacht (she has instant remedy, by herself gybing onto starboard tack, which would give her right of way under rule 37.2).

**A3.4** A starboard-tack yacht running by the lee on a free leg of the course can hold her course and claim right of way (Salcombe YC, RYA 1968/2; IYRU Case 36 refers), provided that she observes rule 35 (Limitation on Altering Course) and, if finally she is forced to gybe she must observe rule 41 (Changing Tacks – Tacking and Gybing).

**A3.5** Yes, the starboard-tack yacht can so alter course, provided that she observes rule 35. The case of *Flamingo* v *Gadfly* (RYA 1971/5; IYRU Case 52) refers.

**A3.6** None, until she is wholly on the pre-start side of the starting line or its extension.

**A3.7** Yes. If, immediately after she has wholly returned, she meets a port-tack yacht which is starting correctly, she must allow the latter ample room and opportunity to keep clear.

**A3.8** Yes.
1. When on a down-wind leg of the course:
   (a) a port-tack yacht has an inside overlap on a starboard-tack yacht; the port-tack yacht can then claim room to round or pass a mark or obstruction. Or
   (b) when a starboard-tack yacht has an inside overlap on a port-tack yacht at a port-hand rounding mark, at which the starboard-tack yacht will have to gybe to round it, she must gybe as soon as she has room to do so.
2. When, after touching a mark, a starboard-tack yacht is re-rounding it to exonerate herself, she must keep clear of all other yachts which are about to round or pass it,

or which have rounded or passed it correctly.

**A3.9** Far enough from S, so that S need not begin to alter course until P has completed her tack, and so that S then has room to keep clear either by luffing or bearing away.

**A3.10** First, the yacht previously holding right of way is under no obligation to anticipate any such change in relationship, and she need not begin to take any avoiding action until the other yacht has established her newly-acquired right of way. Secondly, the yacht which has newly acquired the right of way, must allow the give-way yacht ample room and opportunity to keep clear.

**A4.1** Rule 38.3 says that an overlap which exists between two yachts ... when one or both of them completes a tack or gybe, shall be regarded as a new overlap beginning at that time. If P gybes onto starboard tack while the helmsman of SW is still forward of the Mast Abeam position (SL2SW2), SL may not luff; if she delayed her gybe until SL3, the overlap starts at that moment and she may luff until SW attains Mast Abeam.

**A4.2** No. Rule 43.3(a) says that when the hailed yacht can fetch ... a mark, the hailing yacht shall not be entitled to room to tack and clear the hailed yacht and the hailed yacht shall immediately so inform the hailing yacht.

**A4.3** No. She has not been clear ahead in accordance with rule 38.1.

**A4.4** L is at fault. In the transitional phase, when W is changing from clear ahead to windward yacht, rule 37.3 says that, on establishing an overlap from clear astern, L must allow W ample room and opportunity to keep clear. W may luff head to wind if she pleases.

**A4.5** No. W must immediately try to keep clear. If she delays and, after such delay, contact occurs or L protests, W will be liable to disqualification or to an alternative penalty when so prescribed.

**A4.6**
1. The windward yacht must, when necessary, immediately begin to keep clear.
2. The leeward, right-of-way, yacht must

allow the windward yacht ample room and opportunity to keep clear.

3. The leeward yacht must not sail above her proper course while the overlap exists.

**A4.7**   A proper course is any course which a yacht might sail after the starting signal, in the absence of the other yacht or yachts affected, so as to finish as quickly as possible. The course sailed immediately before luffing or bearing away is presumably, but not necessarily, that yacht's proper course. It was ruled in the appeal *Fundador* v *Ariadne* (RYA 1966/3; IYRU Case 25) that 'When, owing to a difference of opinion on the proper course to be sailed, two yachts on the same tack converge, the windward yacht is bound by the Same Tack – Basic Rule 37.1, to keep clear.' The criterion for a proper course therefore seems to be whether the yacht sailing it has a logical reason for her course, and whether she applies that reason with some consistency.

**A4.8**   Long tradition and unwritten law dictate that the helmsman of a large yacht should, as a matter of courtesy, pass to leeward of a small one to avoid blanketing her and to cause her as little disturbance as possible. Equally, the helmsman of a small yacht should do his utmost to avoid causing a large one to run by the lee and risk an involuntary gybe, especially when she is carrying a spinnaker, and the small yacht should not make a large one tack unless the small one would otherwise run into danger. Nevertheless, when it comes to a pinch, the strict letter of the law must be observed.

**A4.9**   Yes, provided that, in touching her, the leeward yacht does not luff beyond head to wind (when she would begin to tack, within the meaning of the rules) and that no serious damage results.

**A4.10**   Yes. The windward yacht must keep clear.

**A4.11**   No. In light displacement craft it is common practice for the helmsman and crew to move fore and aft according to the course sailed, and such movements come within the limits of normality.

**A4.12**   Yes. The leeward yacht may continue to luff unless the helmsman of the windward yacht hails 'Mast Abeam'.

**A4.13**   The windward yacht fails to respond at her own peril. Under rule 38.4, she may avoid this risk by responding, while reserving the right to protest.

**A5.1**   A yacht begins to gybe when, with the wind aft, the foot of her mainsail crosses her centre line (definition).

**A5.2**   A yacht completes the gybe when her mainsail fills on the other tack (definition).

**A5.3**   When two yachts are both gybing at the same time, the one on the other's port side shall keep clear; rule 41.4. If they are sailing on the same line, so that one is clear astern and dead astern of the other, the yacht clear astern must keep clear.

**A5.4**   A yacht is tacking from the moment she is beyond head to wind (definition); until that moment she is on a tack and luffing.

**A5.5**   When beating to windward, a tack is completed when the yacht has borne away to a close-hauled course; when not beating to windward, to the course on which her mainsail has filled (definition).

**A6.1**   A yacht starts when, after fulfilling her penalty obligations, if any, under rule 51.1(c) (Sailing the Course), and after her starting signal, any part of her hull, crew or equipment first crosses the starting line in the direction of the course to the first mark. Note that the crew and equipment do not have to be in their normal position.

**A6.2**   No. Any luff by L must be carried out slowly and in such a way as to give W room and opportunity to keep clear; this holds good until L has cleared the starting line (rule 40).

**A6.3**   Yes. Although W has been Mast Abeam, she had lost it before the leading yacht started as defined (see A6.1 above). Despite the fact that the overlap was never physically broken, rule 38.3 says that it counts as a new overlap which began when the leading yacht started (at which time W was not Mast Abeam). L may therefore luff, but she is also bound by rule 38.1 and must wait until she has cleared the starting line before she may luff as she pleases.

**A7.1**  No. If she cannot go under S's stern, P should have hailed before she tacked. P is now port-tack yacht and must either bear away to pass astern of S, or she must tack back again – whereupon she may hail S for water under rule 43.1 (if she has enough way on, in order to get about again).

**A7.2**  An outside leeward yacht with luffing rights may take an inside yacht to windward, or to the 'wrong' side, of the mark provided that she hails to that effect and begins to luff before she is within two of her overall lengths of the mark and provided that she also passes to windward of it; rule 42.1(d).

**A7.3**  Rule 35 (Limitations on Altering Course) is mentioned in the note under the heading for Section C; rules 36 (Opposite Tacks – Basic Rule) and 41 (Changing Tacks – Tacking and Gybing) are mentioned in 42.1(c), which deals with yachts on opposite tacks when tacking round a mark.

**A7.4**  A yacht finishes when any part of her hull, crew or equipment in normal position, crosses the finishing line from the direction of the course from the last mark, after fulfilling her penalty obligations, if any, under rule 52.2 (Touching a Mark). Note that a yacht does not have to sail right across the finishing line – she can 'break' it and then drop astern to clear it; she is still racing until she clears the line.

**A8.1**  When two yachts anchor during a race, the one which anchored later shall keep clear; rule 46.1. However, the rule goes on to say specifically that a yacht which is dragging shall keep clear of one which is not.

**A8.2**
(a) Under IYRU basic rule 36, S is starboard-tack yacht and holds right of way.
(b) Under IRPCAS, S ranks as overtaking vessel if she is coming up from more than $22\frac{1}{2}°$ abaft P's beam; S must therefore give way (rule 13).

**A8.3**  P still has right of way. Section (d) of IRPCAS No 13 says 'Any subsequent alteration of the bearing between the two vessels shall not make the overtaking vessel a crossing vessel within the meaning of these Rules or relieve her of her duty of keeping clear of the overtaken vessel *until she is finally past and clear.*' The italics are mine, because I wish to stress the point that, as with the IYRU rules, safety is of paramount importance and must always over-ride any other consideration.

**A9.1**  No. In the first instance, one yacht lodges a protest against another; in the second, the race committee's action under rule 70.2 constitutes a protest against a yacht and is subject to the same procedure.

**A9.2**  The appropriate committee of the national authority can decide, depending on the circumstances of the case, either to dismiss the appeal on the grounds that the appellant, having admitted the infringement, should not escape being penalised owing to a procedural error which did not prejudice his case; to send it back to the protest committee pointing out the error and ordering a new hearing; or to uphold the appeal on the grounds that the improper hearing prejudiced the appellant's case. When appropriate, the second option is preferred because an infringing yacht is then penalised.

**A9.3**  Observers are often used in team racing events. The sailing instructions sometimes prescribe that, when an observer sees what he considers to be a rule infringement, he will blow a whistle or make some other sound signal, to indicate to the competitors that he has seen such an incident. If the alleged infringing yacht does not protest, retire or accept an alternative penalty or, more commonly nowadays, display a green flag, the observer reports the incident to the race committee, which can then act in accordance with rule 70.2 (d).

**A9.4**  No, unless it can be argued that those facts are inadequate or that they are against the weight of evidence. Otherwise, a disqualified yacht can only appeal against a protest committee's irregular hearing of the protest or its interpretation of the rules.

**A9.5**  No, unless the protest committee has failed to forward her appeal within the time limit prescribed by the national authority. The yacht may then inform the national authority of that fact.

**A9.6**    No. It is for the national authority to decide whether or not the appeal is a question of interpretation.

**A9.7**    Onus of satisfying the protest committee is specified in the following rules:

(a)  Rule 41.3 (Onus)

(b)  Rule 42.3(d) (Limitations on Establishing and Maintaining an Overlap in the Vicinity of Marks and Obstructions)

(c)  Rule 42.3(e) (Breaking an Overlap)

(d)  Rule 43.2(b) (iii) (Responding)

In addition, it was ruled in the appeal *Bosun No 56* v *Bosun No 58* (RYA 1973/3) that the onus lies on the windward yacht claiming that she has attained the Mast Abeam position when she hails the leeward yacht to that effect.

**A9.8**    The protest committee must always decide the protest where two yachts collide, since there must have been a rule infringement. When a protest arises from an incident which does not result in a collision, it is open to the protest committee, in the face of lack of evidence or of conflicting evidence, to dismiss the protest on the grounds that the committee is not satisfied that there has been an infringement of any rule.

# Index